"These black proverbs will make you laugh, nod in agreement, remember your grandparents' wise sayings, or simply mutter a heartfelt 'amen.' Crammed with pithy advice, *Lifelines* sheds wisdom on just about every situation from childbirth to adultery to choosing friends. Hallelujah and pass the proverbs."

—Betty DeRamus, author of *Forbidden Fruit: Love Stories from the Underground Railroad* and *Freedom by Any Means: Con Games, Voodoo Schemes, True Love, and Lawsuits on the Underground Railroad*

"*Lifelines* is an indispensable gem to have wherever you are. But most important, it is the lifeline our youths need to buffer their rough edges. What a marvelous gift the authors have compiled for us. Nuff Respect."

—Opal Palmer Adisa, author of *I Name Me Name*

"*Lifelines* is a rich and fascinating exploration into the vast well of African wisdom throughout the centuries. The authors have superbly culled and categorized an exquisite array of ancestral insight and knowledge. This book not only reflects Africa's intellectual contribution to humanity, but it inspires and encourages self-reflection while educating one on history, geography, and social customs. *Lifelines* provides the necessary perspective and clarity we need in these complex times."

—Tony Medina, author of *I and I: Bob Marley*

# Lifelines

# LIFELINES

## The Black Book of Proverbs

Askhari Johnson Hodari

*and*

Yvonne McCalla Sobers

*Illustrations by Katie Yamasaki*

BROADWAY BOOKS

*New York*

BROADWAY

Copyright © 2009 Askhari Johnson Hodari and Yvonne McCalla Sobers

Published in the United States by Broadway Books, an imprint of the
Crown Publishing Group, a division of Random House, Inc., New York.
www.broadwaybooks.com

BROADWAY BOOKS and its logo, a letter B bisected on the diagonal, are
trademarks of Random House, Inc.

Illustrations by Katie Yamasaki

Library of Congress Cataloging-in-Publication Data is available upon request.

ISBN 978-0-7679-3120-5

PRINTED IN THE UNITED STATES OF AMERICA

10 9 8 7 6 5 4 3 2 1

First Edition

For the ancestors whose legacy of proverbs shapes my life.

—YVONNE MCCALLA SOBERS

For the ancestors on whose strong shoulders we stand.
—ASKHARI JOHNSON HODARI

In honor of our past,
and with hope for our future,
we are donating
a portion of our
*Lifelines* royalty proceeds to
Save Africa's Children
(www.saveAfricaschildren.org).

# ✦ CONTENTS

# CHALLENGE · 67

## ETHICS AND VALUES ·

# ✳ FOREWORD

African wit and wisdom are, as they say, proverbial.
Stories and illustrations from the continent and the
African Diaspora confirm the pithiness, earthiness, joy,
and incisive cleverness sown in the African soul. The
stars of fables, Brer Rabbit, and the spider Anansi dis-
play a playful wisdom that is characteristically African.
African proverbs display the same keen observation,
the same shrewd insight, and the same playful wisdom.
*Lifelines: The Black Book of Proverbs* gathers in one place this
essential wisdom from people of African descent.

As an African I am keenly aware of the proverbs
that have girded my own life: "You cannot teach your
grandmother to suck eggs," I was told when, as a smart
young man, I seemed a little "too big for my britches."
"Improve your argument, don't raise your voice," my
father would admonish when passion overtook me. "A
person is a person through other persons" is a truth I
have often repeated. It is a truth that life has taught me
times without number.

I am the person I am because of the relationships
that have formed me and are forming me: the wife

who loves and scolds me, the children who tease and teach me, the grandchildren who draw me into their world, the friends and coworkers who invite me into their lives, who cheer me and challenge me. Without each of them I would not be me.

A proverb is only proverbial if it is true, is useful, and can be readily called to mind and applied. This compendium gathers the insights of the ages in helpful categories that mirror the life cycle. From the stories of their own experiences, the authors offer us illustrations that bring the proverbs to life. We are shown how proverbs may be used to chasten or to praise, to lead, to teach, to guide, or to inspire. We come to recognize that the insight offered in the words of a proverb may offer comfort in times of grief or despair and sew hope into happiness. For every season of life there is a proverb or there are many. Every season of life has been lived before. In the words of proverbs, we see the footprints of those who have gone before us and, perhaps, the shadows of those who will come behind.

Yvonne McCalla Sobers and Askhari Johnson Hodari have offered us a rare treasure. They have created for us a gathering of the elders to offer us wise counsel. They have retained for us a precious strand of the African story in this distillation of African wit and wisdom.

—The Archbishop Desmond Tutu

The tongue of Egyptian experience has the most truth. A lie runs in Cuba only until the truth overtakes it. The tree with the most leaves does not necessarily produce Brazil's juiciest fruit. It is before the drum that a Haitian learns the samba. If you dance with a crocodile in Guyana, you better plan what you're going to do when the dance is done.

As "daughters of experience," we share a passion for proverbs. Short, snappy sayings surround our lives. During our upbringings, we both learned that "a proverb is to speech what salt is to food" (Ethiopia).

When Askhari misbehaved and believed she had gotten away with something, her grandma Addie always said

*All shut eye ain't sleep.*

Grandma also reminded her not to be picky, but that she always had choices, by saying

*Any kind of water puts out a fire.*

Askhari's great aunt Weezy, a proud but poor

woman, used to sit in her rocking chair, cross her legs, and say

*Even a poor rat has at least one hole.*

Askhari's mama, referring to her father's dark complexion, told her

*The blacker the berry, the sweeter the juice.*

Askhari's mama frequently used that proverb to remind Askhari to feel beautiful and to strengthen her children's and students' self-esteem in a white-dominated society.

In Jamaica, Yvonne's mother, like Askhari's mama, warned against premarital sex by saying

*He won't buy the cow if the milk is free.*

Yvonne's mother also warned her that disaster could follow the pleasure of the moment:

*Chicken merry, hawk near.*

Miss Annie, Yvonne's grandmother, cautioned her, in particular, against creating problems where there were none before:

*Trouble don't set up like rain.*

Yvonne's dad advised her always to take responsibility for solving her problems:

*Who have raw meat must seek fire.*

Some of these elders have passed on, but they left us both with words and wisdom collected over centuries. All over the planet, individual experiences have become part of a collective experience: "Proverbs are the daughters of experience" (Sierra Leone). These proverbs provide lifelines that we can grasp in trying to understand and appreciate our world.

Someone once described proverbs as "short sayings based on long experiences." Around the world, people use proverbs to express basic truths in memorable, commonsense form. These proverbs gain credibility through widespread, repeated use.

Adults often use proverbs to give children advice and instruct them on ethics and values. Many parents and grandparents, as well as many spiritual and community leaders, guide young people with messages.

In that same way, people use proverbs to resolve arguments and to solve problems. One proverb even speaks to this point: "A wise man who knows proverbs reconciles difficulties" (Benin). In fact, since "one who applies proverbs gets what she wants" (Zimbabwe), people frequently use proverbs in discussions to add weight to or to support a particular position. Proverbs can also shed light on problems, from the personal to the global.

Proverbs reflect common human experiences as well as unique views of the world. Messages may be similar, but the wisdom of proverbs is often based on setting and experience. European proverbs often refer to oaks, ravens, geese, castles, kingdoms, porridge, and horses. Asian proverbs may speak of flutes, bamboo, roses, and rice. In contrast, African proverbs speak of drums, crocodiles, yams, and gourds.

African elders have kept alive centuries of experience by handing down proverbs by word of mouth. However, much of this wisdom seems in danger of being lost in a world driven more by technology than by collective experience. We intend to preserve African and Africentric proverbs.

*Lifelines* crosses Africa and travels with Africans to all corners of the globe. Readers will find more than two thousand proverbs from more than fifty countries, from about eighty ethnic or linguistic groups. We identify proverbs by country and/or ethnic or language group. The most popular, widely used proverbs are identified by region (West Africa, Caribbean) or continent.

In this collection, we include proverbs that we attribute, without question, to continental or diasporic Africans. We avoided proverbs associated with non-African cultures. Therefore, we excluded proverbs known to be associated with Afrikaans, British, French, or Portuguese settlers in Africa.

We favored proverbs with self-evident meanings that did not need elaboration. We preferred proverbs that seemed likely to offer "lifelines"—lines that can provide our readers with a handhold in the rough weather of life.

Early on, our then editor, Christian, said, "I am not interested in another collection of proverbs arranged alphabetically by theme." He suggested we arrange the proverbs by life cycle, so we began to look at the proverbs as they related to important life events.

These life-cycle events are a part of the natural rhythm of Afridiasporic communities across the world. The proverbs in this book are therefore organized broadly by life cycle: Birth; Childhood; Adolescence, Initiation, and Rites of Passage; Love, Marriage, and Intimacy; Challenge; Ethics and Values; Elderhood; and Death and Afterlife. Within the life-cycle categories, we grouped proverbs by theme. In the Love, Marriage, and Intimacy category, for example, there are proverbs grouped under the themes of friendship, women and men, sex, and home.

We placed proverbs under themes based on our response to the content of a particular proverb. However, our themes are intended more as a guide to the reader than as a classification. We therefore wish readers to consider and reflect on the proverbs beyond the assigned categories and to form their own impressions of each proverb.

Yvonne introduces each section with vignettes that show how events in her own life led her to greater understanding of proverbs, or how proverbs led her to greater understanding of her life. We both speak and understand other languages and dialects, but English is the language we share. For this reason, we included only those proverbs available to us in English. We relied on European translations of African proverbs, so we acknowledge the possibility of shifts in meaning and nuance in the translation process.

Several proverbs are offered in creole, pidgin, patois, and other forms of localized speech. In these cases, we chose to honor and appreciate the rhythm of the people to whom we attributed the selected proverb.

We used our best information to source proverbs

and identify a specific ethnic or language group with which a proverb was associated. We sought to use names of countries and ethnic and language groups used or preferred by African peoples. For example:

- Côte d'Ivoire. "Ivory Coast" is often used in English, but the government prefers the French name, *Côte d'Ivoire*, to be used in all languages.
- Democratic Republic of the Congo (DRC). The country was called the Democratic Republic of the Congo (DRC) in 1964, renamed Zaire in 1971, and again renamed DRC in 1997.
- Igbo. The name of this ethnic group was misspelled "Ibo" by colonial powers.
- Agikuyu. The British colonialists introduced the spellings "Kikuyu" or "Gikuyu."
- Akan, Ashanti, Twi. Twi is a dialect of the Akan language—other Akan dialects include Fante and Akuapem-Twi. Ashanti is one of several geographical areas in which Twi is spoken.
- Mandinka. This term refers to the ethnic groups also known as the Malinke and Mandingo.

In general, proverbs in this collection offer a broad, inclusive view of humanity. However, readers will come across proverbs that demean women and proverbs that exclude women by using male-centered language. We have retained some offensive-sounding proverbs, as we consider them to represent an authentic aspect of African cultures, even though we personally (and politically) disagree with sexist language and concepts.

We are persons who love, live by, and learn from proverbs. We believe in the oral and written tradition of our ancestors. Most essentially, we are people who value, respect, and appreciate Africa and her children, wherever they may be. For a combined total of ten decades, we have been collecting proverbs, and we are pleased to be finally able to share the proverbs in written form.

We hope that you will want to keep *Lifelines* close by to remind yourself of sayings that you may have forgotten; confirm a moral creed you already knew by instinct; and find freedom in truths that may have been buried. "A proverb is the horse of conversation: when the conversation lags, a proverb revives it" (Niger). These proverbs may indeed provide a lifeline, something to grab hold of or refer to in times that require grounding and/or spiritual connection.

Here, in *Lifelines*, we share with readers the wise heart of the motherland and her children. The proverbs on these pages offer inspiration. Guidance. Wisdom. Passion. Inspiration. Strength. Truth. "When the occasion arises, there is a proverb to suit it" (Rwanda, Burundi). Please accept our invitation to *Lifelines* by turning the page.

*Askhari Johnson Hodari*
*Birmingham, Alabama*
*August 2009*

*Yvonne McCalla Sobers*
*Kingston, Jamaica*
*August 2009*

Lifelines

Birth

I went to Ghana as a young bride in 1960. As the first year passed, I saw the eyes of my Ga community grow more questioning because my stomach remained flat. What was I waiting for? Surely I had to know the South African proverb that "to give birth is to lengthen one's knees."

When my pregnancy arrived, it did not remain unnoticed for long. "A fire and a pregnancy cannot be kept secret" (Rwanda). Even before my first medical checkup, I seemed to be outgrowing my clothes. I could no longer tolerate the smell of smoked fish in the delicious groundnut stews my Ga friends gave me, but I had to have *kelewele* (fried plantains) at meals and between meals.

My Ga community now surprised me with their attention. They had called me *oboruni* (literally "one from over the horizon"), the same term used for whites. They had considered me an outsider because I could produce no memory of a village, a language, or a family name to affirm my identity as African. With my pregnancy evident, I felt embraced by aunts and uncles, sisters and brothers everywhere. Market vendors gave their blessings along with their best yams (and sometimes their best prices as well).

When I was six months pregnant, tests showed I was

carrying twins. In the early 1960s, Ga communities assumed that many babies would die, so they placed special value on twin births.

My Jamaican blood family and the friends of my childhood were an ocean away when my babies were born. However, I had no doubt that I had given my twins the gift of roots in the Ga community. "The bird flies, but always returns to earth" (Senegal, Gambia).

# ❈ ORIGIN

There is nothing that has no origin. —Kenya (Agikuyu)

Every cackling hen was an egg at first. —Rwanda

There is no bird that does not know eggs.

—Namibia (Ovambo)

The bird flies but always
returns to earth.

—Senegal, Gambia (Wolof)

A bird may die in the sky, but
its bones must reach the
ground. —Africa

Everything above falls to earth
at the end. —Niger, Nigeria

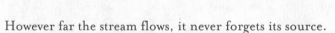

When you see an old bone on
the highway, remember it was
once covered with flesh.

—Haiti

However far the stream flows, it never forgets its source.

—Nigeria (Yoruba)

Good fruit comes from good seed. —Mozambique (Tsonga)

A child in the mother's womb unfailingly takes some
qualities from her. —Uganda (Ganda)

Marrow is the father of blood. —Benin, Nigeria, Togo (Yoruba)

When a yam does not grow well, we do not blame the yam; it is because of the soil.

*—Ghana*

A man's urine will always fall near him.

*—Angola*

The antelope does not bear a child that cannot run.

*—Niger, Nigeria (Hausa)*

Warm water never forgets that it was once cold.

*—Nigeria*

To return to the same thing is not foolishness.

*—Kenya (Agikuyu)*

Everything a house gets is by favor of the door.

*—Niger, Nigeria (Hausa)*

If you do not know where you are going, you should know where you came from.

*—United States (South Carolina Gullah)*

## ⸎ PREGNANCY AND CHILDBIRTH

Let a female develop her breast; one day, she must give it to her child.

*—Nigeria (Igbo)*

A fire and a pregnancy cannot be kept secret.

*—Rwanda*

He who longs too much for a child will marry a pregnant woman.

*—Mali (Bambara)*

The pregnant woman is not afraid of her husband's penis.

*—Angola, Namibia*

One does not force a pregnant woman to give birth.

*—Côte d'Ivoire (Baule)*

Whatever a pregnant woman says is said by two people.
—*Benin, Nigeria, Togo (Yoruba)*

To give birth is to lengthen one's knees.
—*South Africa (Zulu)*

During childbirth, a pregnant woman does not hide her vagina.
—*Africa*

You cannot abort the pregnancy of a born child.
—*Africa*

Childbirth will later lighten your burden.
—*Namibia*

Give birth to children and you will be pregnant with worries.
—*Namibia*

## ❧ NAMING

A person takes his name with him wherever he goes.
—*Ghana*

One's name is one's most effective advocate abroad.
—*Benin, Nigeria, Togo (Yoruba)*

A name or nickname influences one's character.
—*Benin, Nigeria, Togo (Yoruba)*

A good name shines in the dark.
—*Tanzania (Zanzibar)*

Happiness and a pure name are fragile things.

—Benin, Nigeria, Togo (Yoruba)

The purity of your name is worth more than the purity of your body.

—Tunisia

The worst you can do to a man is to break his name.

—East Africa (Kiswahili)

In order to find out evildoers, every human being is given a name.

—Ghana (Twi)

The owner of a name knows his name; you say to the thief, "Stop, thief!" and he bolts.

—Niger, Nigeria (Hausa)

If you inherit a name, you must also adopt its affairs.

—Africa

A not-so-good-looking child is given a beautiful name.

—Ethiopia

The stream may dry up, but the watercourse retains its name.

—Benin, Nigeria, Togo (Yoruba)

If you have spoiled your name at home, go and live elsewhere.

—DRC

It is not what you are called, but what you answer to.

—Africa

Rivers dry up, but not their names.

—Benin, Nigeria, Togo (Yoruba)

One's name remains above the grave.

—Ethiopia

# Childhood

With just the baby manual of the day to guide me, I underestimated the work of caring for twin babies. My blood family was an entire day's flight away, and telephone connection between Jamaica and Ghana was all but nonexistent in the early 1960s.

One night someone knocked on my door just as I was dashing to grab an hour's sleep before our babies woke up for another round of changing and feeding and burping and changing again. The visitor was a neighbor whom I knew by sight, and she brought a woman named Afua to my home. The neighbor explained that Afua would help me with our babies. I sensed the community had already recruited and selected Afua, leaving me with just the option to hire. "It takes a village to raise a child" (Nigeria).

Afua started to work the following morning. She spoke no English and I spoke no Ga. However, we communicated in a language that demanded that we give full attention to each other's eyes and gestures. I showed her what to do, and she responded by following my instructions exactly. If she had a better idea, she would show me. We never argued because, as the Namibians say, "He who does not speak does not argue."

I relied on Afua's experience as a mother to protect

our babies. I also knew she brought to her tasks the child-rearing wisdom of the Ga community. About one in six children in the Ga community and in different parts of Africa died before the child's fifth birthday. Afua's facial marks were evidence of siblings that had died before she was born, so I knew she would be very sensitive to the truth of the Malawian proverb "A newly arrived chicken is vulnerable to eagles."

Sometimes Afua went to unusual lengths to shelter our babies from the possibility of harm. One mid-morning I missed her, and by midday I was fuming, because an all-day power outage was adding to the stress of my not being able to account for her absence. Afua returned with a charcoal iron, a collectible even at that time. Normally, she would iron our babies' laundry, since flies laid larvae on clothes hung outdoors to dry. The larvae hatched on contact with human skin, creating a painful boil that would turn out to be a fully grown maggot under the skin. For Afua, absence of electricity was no excuse for risking harm to babies whom she considered as much hers as mine. "The mother is she who catches the knife by the blade" (Botswana, South Africa).

When our babies were about eighteen months old, I felt confident enough about their welfare to return to my teaching job. Afua and I were still holding conversations without relying on words, but our babies knew she was more than family.

I lost touch with Afua when I left Ghana, but she remains in my mind always, because "he who takes a child by the hand takes a mother by the heart" (Africa).

# ⁂ PARENTS AND PARENTING

Parents give birth to the body of their children, but not always to their characters. —*Uganda (Ganda)*

Bearing a child is different from rearing it.
—*Kenya (Agikuyu)*

It takes a village to raise a child. —*Nigeria*

A mother is not to be compared with another person—she is incomparable. —*DRC (Mongo)*

The rich relative is not greater than the mother.
—*Ghana*

At feeding time, every calf knows its mother. —*Africa*

The breast of your mother is not to be forgotten.
—*Africa*

Every animal knows how to suckle its baby.
—*Kenya (Agikuyu)*

A hen never tread on her chicken too hard. —*Jamaica*

A mother never bites her child to the bone. —*Haiti*

When a child bites into his mother's breast, he is denied milk. —*Africa*

The infant sucks only what it finds in its mother's breasts. —*Senegal, Gambia (Wolof)*

The baby who refuses its mother's breast will never be fully grown.

*—Kenya (Agikuyu)*

No man will starve in his mother's house.

*—Liberia*

A motherly woman knows what her child will eat.

*—Ghana (Akan)*

When a woman is hungry, she says, "Roast something for the children that they may eat."

*—Africa*

A child's fingers are not scalded by a piece of hot yam that his mother puts into his palm.

*—Africa*

The chicken with children does not swallow the worm.

*—Tanzania (Sukuma)*

A cow gave birth to a fire; she wanted to lick it, but it burned; she wanted to leave it, but she could not because it was her own child.

*—Ethiopia*

A mother's tears are no hard work.

*—DRC (Mongo)*

If a child takes interest in crying, its mother will develop interest in comforting it.

*—Benin, Nigeria, Togo (Yoruba)*

The child who isn't crying has no need to be nursed.

*—Haiti*

No child should be babied while another is offered to the hyena to bite.

*—Kenya*

To his mother, a baby monkey is the most beautiful creature
in the world.                                             —*Ethiopia*

A cow never runs away from her calves.        —*Zambia (Bemba)*

Only lay hold of a child, and you will see its mother.
                                                          —*DRC (Mongo)*

The mother is she who catches the knife by the blade.
                                           —*Botswana, South Africa (Tswana)*

One does not bypass a mother to bury her child.
                                                          —*Ghana (Akan)*

He who takes anything to his mother never says it
is too heavy.                                        —*Uganda (Ganda)*

Even if you hate your mother, you do not hand her
over to the enemy.                                   —*Ghana (Twi)*

Your mother is still your mother, though her legs be
small.                                            —*Malawi (Chewa)*

A wife is for a certain time, your mother is for always.
                                                          —*Haiti*

A mother cannot die.                              —*DRC (Mongo)*

Were it not for the mother, a child would not know its
father.                                                   —*Africa*

If you know the father and grandfather, do not worry
about the son.                                            —*Africa*

As long as I am running, my father will still have a son.
                                                          —*Brazil*

When you follow in the path of your father, you learn to walk like him.
—*Ghana*

Even though you may be taller than your father, you are still not his equal.
—*Africa*

The child who does not listen to his father never grows old.
—*Uganda (Iteso)*

When a father beats his child, he is likely to beat also its mother.
—*Uganda (Ganda)*

Do not beat the mother if you love the child.
—*DRC (Tetela)*

The most important thing a father can do for his children is to love their mother.
—*Africa*

Who loves the mother must love the child.
—*Zambia (Bemba)*

If you support your wife, you also support your child.
—*Ghana*

If you are strict with your children, you will be respected.
—*Ghana*

To bring up children by spoon-feeding will bring up lazy ones.
—*Mozambique*

A child who is to be successful is not reared exclusively on a bed of down.
—*Ghana*

You do not mind if the child you are sending is going
with a cheerful face or not.                    —*Ghana (Twi)*

A parent who excuses a child's ways makes the child
a thief.                                        —*Africa*

If your child is dancing clumsily, you say, "You are a
clumsy dancer." You do not say, "Darling, do as
you please."                                    —*Ghana (Twi)*

However high you lift the kid, place it gently on
the ground.                                     —*Ghana (Twi)*

If your neighbor comes to your house with an
unmannerly child, do not defer to the child or he
will tear your hat to pieces.                   —*Ghana (Twi)*

Let the parents punish the child.               —*Africa*

A child who lacks home training will be trained
in public.                                      —*Africa*

A parent bears the body but does not bear the spirit.
                                    —*East Africa (Kiswahili)*


## ❊ CHILDREN AND YOUTH

Youth is beauty, even in cattle.                —*Egypt*

If a man leaves little children behind him,
it is as if he did not die.                     —*Morocco*

A new daughter is many voices.                  —*Kenya (Agikuyu)*

Who brings forth a daughter also gets a son.

—*Uganda (Ganda)*

A child is like a precious stone, but also a heavy burden.

—*East Africa (Kiswahili)*

A newly arrived chicken is vulnerable to eagles.

—*Malawi (Yawo)*

The birds are caught while still fledgling.

—*South Africa (Zulu)*

You can bend a tree or orient its course only
when it is very young.

—*Cameroon*

No child is born with teeth.

—*Africa*

By crawling, a child learns to stand.

—*Niger, Nigeria (Hausa)*

Children learn to creep where they can learn to go.

—*Haiti*

When a child has climbed a tree a little way, he will
come down again.

—*Ghana*

If you haven't reached the age of wearing big beads,
you do not thread them.

—*Ghana (Akan)*

A chicken egg cannot turn over its hen.

—*Africa*

The younger should not intrude into the seat
of the elders.

—*Benin, Nigeria, Togo (Yoruba)*

No one sends a child on an errand and gets angry
with him if he does not do it well.

—*Ghana (Akan)*

A boy is not sent to collect the honey.     *—Kenya*

The child who bites the back of his mother will find
no other willing to carry him.     *—Nigeria (Yoruba)*

It is a bad child who does not take advice.

*—Ghana (Ashanti)*

The son disgraces his father by bad conduct.     *—Morocco*

When a child cries, we do not tie him to a log.

*—Ghana (Akan)*

A child who denies its mother a night's sleep will
also remain awake.     *—Gambia*

A child who cries often makes it difficult for people
to know when it has been beaten.     *—Africa*

When your child pretends to be dying, then you pretend
to be making preparations for his funeral.     *—Ghana*

As the child has not seen what happened before his birth,
let him be satisfied with having it told to him.

*—Ghana, Benin, Togo (Ewe)*

Children have wide ears and long tongues.     *—Haiti*

What the child says, he has heard at home.

*—Senegal, Gambia (Wolof)*

A man fights with his wife but not with his child.

*—Ghana*

A child who cannot hold the handle of a sword firmly
cannot ask who killed his father.     *—Africa*

If youthful pride were wealth, then every man has had it
in his lifetime.
—*Ghana (Twi)*

The trees that are growing are tomorrow's forest.
—*Zambia (Bemba)*

Children are dear to the heart and dear to the purse.
—*South Africa*

It is not difficult to find a gift for a child.
—*Africa*

When you show a child the moon, she sees only
your finger.
—*Ghana (Akan)*

No one needs to show a child God.
—*Ghana (Akan)*

If children see an eagle that has been beaten by the rain,
they say it is a vulture.
—*Ghana (Akan)*

Even a child can think. Some do it rather well.
—*South Africa*

You must agree with the youth if you associate with them.
—*Kenya (Agikuyu)*

Do not stop children having fun; otherwise they will
also stop your serious work.
—*Gambia (Mandinka)*

Twenty children cannot play together for twenty years.
—*Africa*

The children of the same mother do not always agree.
—*Senegal, Gambia (Wolof)*

He who takes a child by the hand takes a mother
by the heart.
                                                    —*Africa*

Children are no more separable from their parents
than the stripes from the zebra.
                                                    —*Angola*

It is the duty of children to wait on elders,
and not the elders on children.
                                                    —*Kenya*

One gives birth to one's children; one buys one's slave
in the market.
                                        —*Benin, Nigeria, Togo (Yoruba)*

No child cuts his finger in cutting meat for his father or
mother.
                                                    —*Kenya (Agikuyu)*

Youth is hope; old age is remembrance.      —*East Africa (Kiswahili)*

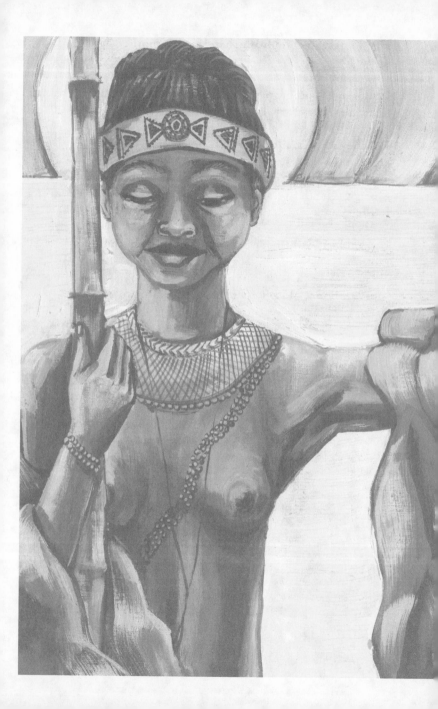

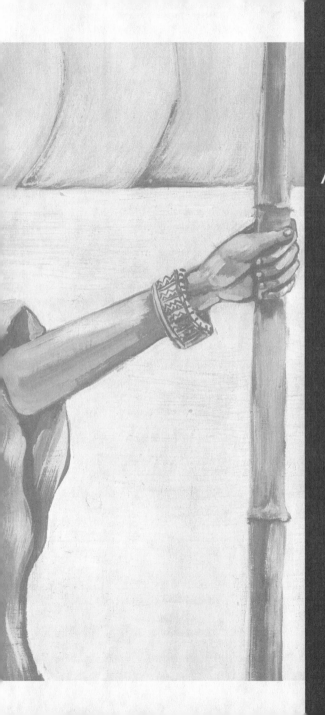

Adolescence,
Initiation,
and
Rites of
Passage

My African friends and I came of age in different ways. Their initiation process was explicit, setting out specific roles for men and women. My entry into adulthood felt more ad hoc, leaving some room to explore, but many practical questions remained unanswered.

I sensed the nervousness of my elders when my monthly periods started. I received warnings of social expectations (mostly unspecified) because "bats who think they are birds are in for a great surprise" (Africa). Since my elders regarded me as a young woman, I was no longer supposed to play contact games with boys. Moreover, I needed to guard my social position by not being too friendly with the girl down the road who had too many visiting "uncles." At the same time, my elders saw me as a child who should not act too grown up, since "the bird is not big until he spreads his wings" (Liberia).

My community also looked to church and school to help me to adapt to adulthood: "You change your steps according to the change in the rhythm of the drum" (Ghana).

If I had belonged to an African or Africentric community, my elders would have isolated my age-mates and me. They would have instructed us on sex, cooking, marriage, birth control, and living our lives according to the ethics and values of the community. Elders would also have taught us to value silence: "The eyes are for seeing, the ears for hearing, and the lips to shut up" (Haiti). They would also have helped us to learn to control our emotions, because "the roaring lion kills no game" (Tanzania).

Despite the "talk" I received when my period came, the church catechism I learned, and the schoolbooks I studied, I still had to discover on my own how to prevent rice from burning, a baby from crying all night, or a husband from staying out all night.

My most meaningful initiation into adulthood came when I learned what African elders teach initiates at the outset: "Education is life, not books" (Kiswahili).

# ❋ QUIET, SILENCE, AND STILLNESS

Even silence speaks.　　　　　　　　　　　　*—Niger, Nigeria (Hausa)*

Silence is more than just a lack of words.　　　　*—Egypt*

Silence conceals foolishness.　　　　　　　　*—Egypt*

Silence is the best answer to the stupid.　　　*—Egypt*

Not everything good to eat,
good to talk.　　　　*—Jamaica*

One who talks thinks; one who
keeps silent thinks more.

　　　　　　*—Uganda (Ganda)*

He who does not speak does
not argue.　　　*—Namibia (Ovambo)*

Silence does not bring harm.

　　　　　*—East Africa (Kiswahili)*

Silence defeats the
scandalmonger.　*—Niger, Nigeria (Hausa)*

Better to be silent than to speak ill of another.

　　　　　　　　　　*—Niger, Nigeria (Hausa)*

The lion that moves silently is the one that eats the meat.

　　　　　　　　　　*—East Africa (Kiswahili)*

The roaring lion kills no game.　　　　　　*—Tanzania*

However pleasant the sound of a drum, silence is better.

—*Niger, Nigeria (Hausa)*

The eyes are for seeing, the ears for hearing, and the lips to shut up.

—*Haiti*

However sweet is talk, silence is better.

—*West Africa (Fulani)*

## ❋ IDENTITY AND INDIVIDUALITY

Whoever the sun shines on will bask in it and be easily identified by it.

—*Ethiopia*

The gazelle jumps, and should her child crawl?

—*West Africa (Fulfulde)*

A cat may go to a monastery, but she still remains a cat.

—*Ethiopia*

Bats who think they are birds are in for a great surprise.

—*Africa*

There is no partridge that does not have its own way of scratching the ground.

—*Kenya (Agikuyu)*

Let each bird cry according to its kind.

—*Niger, Nigeria (Hausa)*

You can recognize a person's tribe by the way he cries.

—*United States (South Carolina Gullah)*

Cutting the ears of a mule will not make him a horse.

—*United States (Louisiana Creole)*

Nobody walks with another man's gait.

—*Kenya*

Even if made of gold, shoes are still for the feet.     —*Ethiopia*

If you are a peg, endure the knocking; if you are a
mallet, strike.
                                                        —*Morocco*

## ✳ CHANGE AND ADAPTABILITY

When thrown into the sea, the stone said, "After all, this
is also a home."
                                                        —*Uganda (Ganda)*

If a crocodile deserts the water, it does not die.
                                                        —*East Africa (Kiswahili)*

The road does not stop a bird.
                                                        —*Ghana (Akan)*

Even the Niger River must flow around an island.

—*Nigeria*

To a man who has only a hammer in his tool kit,
every problem looks like a nail.

—*Africa*

If you have run out of gunpowder, use your gun
as a club.

—*Nigeria*

If you find no fish, you have to eat bread.

—*Ghana*

Don't hang all your clothes on one nail.

—*Barbados*

The bird is not big until he spreads his wings.

—*Liberia (Jabo)*

No one grows up to eat a mouse.

—*Ghana (Akan)*

When the baby grows, the crying changes.

—*Nigeria (Annang)*

When a bird is in a snare, its cry is peculiar.

—*Ghana (Twi)*

The woman who grows too big for her underwear
will soon dance naked.

—*Africa*

You change your steps according to the change in
the rhythm of the drum.

—*Ghana (Ewe)*

If a European is in need, he speaks Twi.

—*Ghana (Akan)*

The chameleon changes color to match the earth;
the earth does not change color to match the chameleon.

—*West Africa*

The sun does not change, but the clouds do.

—*Africa*

It is possible for the owners of a house to warm
themselves when their house is on fire. —*Kenya (Agikuyu)*

The wind does not break a tree that bends.
—*Tanzania (Sukuma)*

If we do not bend, we do not lie down. —*Ghana (Akan)*

## ❋ EDUCATION

If you learn while young, you can do it when old.
—*South Africa*

Instruction in youth is like engraving in stones.
—*North Africa (Berber)*

A burnt child dreads the fire. —*Lesotho*

The child says nothing but what he heard at the fireside.
—*Haiti*

A home is the school for morals. —*Africa*

If you carry your baby and you steal, you show it how
to do so. —*Uganda (Ganda)*

Choking will teach you to chew properly; falling will
teach you to walk properly. —*Madagascar (Malagasy)*

A tree that does not know how to dance will be taught
by the wind. —*Africa*

As the crab is near the stream, it understands the
language of the stream. —*Ghana (Twi)*

If the poet does not teach his song to the people, who will sing it?
—*Tanzania (Zanzibar)*

It is before the drum one learns to know the samba.
—*Haiti*

No archer is born with a bow.
—*Africa*

You cannot learn all the hunter's tricks in one day.
—*Africa*

Learning is like sailing the ocean: no one has ever seen it all.
—*East Africa (Kiswahili)*

Education is the work of your entire life.
—*Haiti*

Learn with the left hand while you still have the right one.
—*Namibia*

He who learns teaches.
—*Ethiopia*

Not everything scholar know he learn from teacher.
—*Barbados*

A student does not know about masterhood, but a master knows about studenthood.
—*West Africa (Mandinka)*

Education is life, not books.
—*East Africa (Kiswahili)*

A wise man without a book is like a workman without tools.
—*Morocco*

As long as a human being lives, he will learn.
—*Libya*

Love,
Marriage, and
Intimacy

I grew up in Jamaica with the dream of meeting Mr. Right, marrying him, and living happily ever after. Friends from West Africa showed me other ways of looking at love and marriage.

Elizabeth and Andrew considered themselves modern, dating, courting, and marrying according to Eurocentric traditions. However, Andrew's mother did not approve of her son's marriage to a "foreigner." Her main concern was that the two sets of extended families had not played the traditional role in matching the couple, and so had missed the opportunity for bonding. "Birds that drink water at one swamp know each other's feathers" (Malawi). Most of all, Andrew's mother was worried that notions of romantic love would not be enough to keep the marriage afloat, because "one who marries for love alone will have bad days but good nights" (Egypt). When the couple's first child was born, Andrew's mother felt somewhat appeased. As a Malawian proverb states, "A child is the girdle of marriage."

My colleague Kwabena was in an arranged marriage. When his oldest uncle died, he married his uncle's wife to protect the widow and helped raise her children. He had done his duty at the cost of completing a university degree, but he was satisfied with having honored the wishes of his departed uncle, because "kinship is like the scales; it keeps one on balance" (Malawi).

Onyeka is a Nigerian woman with an Ivy League doctorate and Boston-tinged accent. She views Western-style marriage as based on women's looks, when "beauty is half a God-given favor, intelligence a whole one" (West Africa). Traditional forms of African polygamy, she says, can resolve marital strains that could otherwise lead to divorce. Her mother assisted her father in choosing other wives when she grew weary of his demands. Onyeka's mother was able to retain the social and financial benefits of marriage, while gaining sisterhood support and help with house chores and conjugal duties.

In Onyeka's opinion, monogamy places ambitious women at a disadvantage. It confines them, forcing them to postpone or cancel their life goals. "A bad marriage ruins a good woman" (Ghana). On the other hand, she argues that polygamy can allow women to be as free as if they were single (earning degrees and pursuing careers), while having the status of married women.

Onyeka, Kwabena, Elizabeth, and Andrew had different approaches to love and marriage. However, they all saw marriage as an important means of broadening and deepening family connections, because "relatives are a better defense than a fortress" (Angola).

## ❈ FAMILY AND KINSHIP

Oneness through blood cannot be severed.

*—Kenya (Agikuyu)*

Water does run, but blood does clot.      *—Barbados*

One cannot leave one's clan or family.      *—Kenya (Agikuyu)*

The family is like the forest. If you are outside, it is
dense; if you are inside, you see each tree has its own
position.      *—Nigeria, Ghana*

The family tree isn't cut.      *—Ghana (Akan)*

The berry don't fall far from the tree.

*—Barbados, Trinidad and Tobago*

Kinship cannot be washed with water and removed.

*—Mozambique, Zimbabwe (Shona), Ghana*

Kinship is like the scales; it keeps one in balance.

*—Ethiopia*

The compassion of a people is cultivated at a
grandmother's knee.      *—Zimbabwe*

A cousin does not ask and isn't refused anything.

*—Kenya (Agikuyu)*

One cannot hear a brother's cry and say one is busy.

*—Nigeria (Igbo)*

A brother is like one's shoulder.      *—Somalia*

A brother is the eye on the back of the head.

*—Uganda (Ganda, Lugbara)*

There is no brother in the family except the brother
who is kindhearted. *—Egypt*

When your brother cannot give you milk, he begs it from
others for you. *—Uganda (Ganda)*

If your brother is up the plum tree, you will eat the
best plum. *—Africa*

Impatience with your brother is in the flesh; it does not
reach the bone. *—Burkina Faso (Mamprusi)*

Brothers must not quarrel over an acre.

*—Kenya, Tanzania (Maasai)*

A dispute between brothers does not have to be settled by
the chief. *—Kenya, Tanzania (Maasai)*

You can choose your friends, but not your brother or
sister. *—Africa*

A faithful friend is never better than a sister.

*—Nigeria (Igbo)*

If your sister is in the group of singing girls, your name
won't be lost. *—Ghana (Akan)*

When your sister does your hair, you do not need
a mirror. *-Africa*

Anger toward a sister is only flesh deep, not bone deep.

*—Nigeria (Igbo)*

Relatives are a better defense than a fortress.

—Angola (Umbundu)

The family is an army.                                    —Africa

If relatives help one another, what harm can be done
to them?                                                 —Ethiopia

A distant relative can help you cross a river.           —Ethiopia

It is the person whose name you bear that you bathe
in the same water with.                              —Ghana (Akan)

Things of the family should not be escorted outside the
boundary of the homestead.                        —Kenya (Agikuyu)

If a member of a family or clan is lost, he is called back
by the horn of the clan.                            —Ghana (Twi)

Do not abandon your family and friends for strangers.

—Haiti

## ❊ FRIENDSHIP

Good friend better than pocket money.           —Belize, Jamaica

Better to lose a little money than a little friendship.

—Madagascar (Malagasy)

A friend is the one who praises you when you are
not there.                              —Benin, Nigeria, Togo (Yoruba)

Friendship makes me dine in a friend's house when I
have enough to eat in my own home.                    —Nigeria

To give to your friend isn't to cast away; it is to store for
the future.
*—East Africa (Kiswahili)*

A stone from the hand of a friend is an apple.    *—Morocco*

To be without a friend is to be poor for true.    *—Jamaica*

Friendship does not need pepper to cry.    *—Congo*

Crying is useless if you have no friends who will listen.
*—Angola*

Not to aid a friend in his time of distress is to kill him
in your heart.    *—Africa*

If you wish to retain a friend for long, do not demand
too much and do show your own considerate acts.
*—Ethiopia*

A little service out of friendship is worth more than a
great service that is forced.    *—Uganda (Ganda)*

A friend only in words can be found anyplace.    *—Ethiopia*

The fact that people visit you often does not make them
your friends.    *—Haiti*

Just because someone is smiling at you does not mean he
or she is your friend.    *—Haiti*

One who gets tired of an old friendship will also get tired
of a new one.    *—Uganda (Ganda)*

If you are careful with your enemy once, be careful with
your friend a thousand times.    *—East Africa (Kiswahili)*

If you want to know your friend, lay down on the roadside and pretend to be drunk. *—Jamaica*

When you are in trouble, you see your real friends. *—Ghana (Twi)*

A broken friendship may be mended but never made completely whole. *—Benin, Nigeria, Togo (Yoruba)*

A person who befriends another should make allowances for quarrels. *—Benin, Nigeria, Togo (Yoruba)*

A friend has patience with you even when you are angry. *—East Africa (Kiswahili)*

Friendship doubles joy and halves grief. *—Egypt*

The best friends are the old ones. *—Egypt*

A friend who would die with one is rare; he who would do so accompanies one even to war. *—Benin, Nigeria, Togo (Yoruba)*

Genuine love and friendship is like hot charcoal that is covered by ashes; when you return to it much later and poke it a little, it is rekindled and reactivated anew. *—Africa*

## WOMEN AND MEN

Bread without sauce and a home without a wife are meaningless. *—Africa*

A woman is to man what food is to the stomach. *—Ethiopia*

A woman is a basket of flour; the hungry come of their own accord.
*—Angola (Umbundu)*

Women are the best promoters of the young fruit of the lemon tree.
*—Ghana*

A woman is more than her breasts; goats also have two.
*—Rwanda*

Often a woman struggles to be a person, not just a female.
*—Ethiopia*

Queen rule beehive, not king.
*—Guyana*

Better a bad wife than an empty house.
*—Côte d'Ivoire*

The man is the central pole of the house.
*—Uganda (Ganda), DRC (Lugbara)*

One who seeks a wife does not speak contemptuously of women.
*—Ghana (Ashanti)*

Women and sky cannot be understood.
*—Kenya (Agikuyu)*

Women are like the bullets of a revolver; one comes out the barrel, and another one is ready in the cylinder.
*—Brazil*

The woman is cold water that kills you, deep water that you drown in.
*—Nigeria*

A woman is like a shield: you call it light until you try it on.
*—Uganda (Ganda)*

What was hatched a hen must not try to be a rooster.
*—Grenada, Tobago*

A woman is like a blanket: if you cover yourself with it, it bothers you; if you throw it aside, you will feel the cold.

*—Ghana*

If a woman gets rich, she changes into a man.     *—Ghana*

With tender words you have less luck with a woman than with jewels.

*—North Africa (Berber)*

A woman's clothes are the price her husband pays for peace.

*—Central Africa, East Africa, southern Africa (Bantu)*

Man strength is in he hand. Woman strength is in she mouth.

*—Barbados*

A bad marriage ruins a good woman.     *—Ghana (Akan)*

The folly of a man isn't broadcast like that of a woman.

*—Africa*

A woman is like the earth: everyone sits down on her.

*—DRC (Lingala)*

Very few males are as kind to children as females; it is the females who recall the labor pains.     *—Tanzania (Haya)*

No man is a hero to his woman.     *—East Africa (Kiswahili)*

A man isn't a pillow for a woman to lay her head on.

*—Ghana (Akan)*

Man is like palm wine: when young, sweet but without strength; in old age, strong but harsh.     *—Congo*

There is no popular young man without a fault.

*—South Africa (Zulu)*

When the men have left the village, the women will bathe outside.
—*Côte d'Ivoire (Baule)*

Pride and dignity would belong to women if only men would leave them alone.
—*Egypt*

A female tongue gets things more easily than a strong man.
—*Ghana (Akan)*

Resourcefulness is to a woman what serenity is to nightfall.
—*Ethiopia*

If you educate a man, you educate an individual, but if you educate a woman, you educate a nation.
—*Ghana (Fante)*

## ❋ BEAUTY AND APPEARANCE

Everyone has God-given beauty.
—*Ghana (Akan)*

Beauty is half a God-given favor; intelligence is a whole one.
—*West Africa (Fulani)*

A man possesses beauty in his quality, and a woman possesses quality in her beauty.
—*Cuba*

A lovely face does not need adornment.
—*East Africa (Kiswahili)*

A woman's beauty isn't in her face.
—*Tanzania*

Beauty is an empty calabash.
—*Burundi*

Orange yellow, but you no know if he sweet.

—Guyana, Barbados

Beauty without grace is like rose without smell.

—Benin, Nigeria, Togo (Yoruba)

Beauty does not pay debts.

—Ghana (Akan)

Good looks cannot carry to the shop.

—Barbados

A set of white teeth does not indicate a pure heart.

—Nigeria

Pepper has a beautiful face with an ugly temper.

—Africa

Beautiful woman, beautiful trouble.

—Jamaica

An attractive person cannot be without blemish—if he does not steal, he bewitches.

—Zambia

The face of water is beautiful, but it is not good to sleep on.

—Ghana (Ashanti)

Even the handsome are divorced.

—Egypt

A nice navel does not prevent a girl from suffering.

—Burundi (Rundi)

The dog with lovely eyes may be a good hunter or a thief.

—Africa

Beautiful, big eyes sting sharper than lemons.

—Cuba

A beautiful thing is never perfect.

—Egypt

True love isn't in the mirror; it is in the heart.

*—East Africa (Kiswahili)*

The heart sees farther than the head.

*—Africa*

What is in the heart will lead to the mouth.

*—West Africa (Fulani), Ethiopia*

When the heart gives orders, the body becomes its slave.

*—Niger, Nigeria (Hausa)*

He who loves you loves you with your dirt.

*—Uganda (Ganda)*

A lover is unmindful of any charcoal on the body.

*—Nigeria (Annang)*

Who wants a thing is blind to its faults.

*—Egypt*

People who love each other do not dwell on each other's mistakes.

*—Kenya (Agikuyu)*

Love is like a seed: it does not choose the ground on which it falls.

*—South Africa (Zulu)*

Love is like young rice: transplanted, still it grows.

*—Africa*

Love is like a baby: it needs to be treated tenderly.

*—Congo*

Hearts do not meet each other like roads.

*—Côte d'Ivoire*

Love is like a cough; it cannot be hidden.

—Tanzania (Zanzibar)

The heart isn't a knee that can be bent.       —Senegal

The one who loves an unsightly person is the one who
makes him beautiful.       —Uganda (Ganda)

Truth should be in love and love in truth.

—East Africa (Kiswahili)

Where there is love there is no darkness.       —Burundi

Love does not listen to rumors.       —Ghana (Akan)

If I have decided to love somebody, I oblige myself to be
patient with him/her.       —Tanzania

Love has to be shown by deeds, not words.

—East Africa (Kiswahili)

Love does not get lost on its way home.       —Africa

To be smiled at isn't to be loved.       —Kenya (Agikuyu)

You shake man hand but you do not shake him heart.

—Jamaica

The teeth may smile, but the heart does not forget.

—Uganda (Ganda)

Heart do not mean everything mouth say.

—United States (South Carolina Gullah)

Lip kiss no touch the heart.       —Jamaica

Dogs do not love people; they love the place where they are fed.
—*Burundi*

A tree knot spoils the ax; hunger spoils love.
—*Nigeria (Efik)*

Thought breaks the heart.
—*Cameroon*

Quick to love, quick not to love.
—*Nigeria*

Do not hurry to love someone. Perhaps she hates you. Do not hurry to hate her. Perhaps she loves you.
—*West Africa (Fulfulde)*

It isn't enough to love if you are not loved in return.
—*Mozambique (Tsonga)*

Loving one who does not love you is loving the rain that falls in the forest.
—*Rwanda*

The ailment of the heart is known to only one.
—*South Africa (Zulu)*

If a woman does not love you, she calls you brother.
—*Côte d'Ivoire (Baule)*

Mutual love is often better than natural brotherhood.
—*Congo, Angola (Bakongo)*

Let your love be like a misty rain, coming softly but flooding the river.
—*Madagascar*

May your love not be like stone: if it breaks, you cannot put the pieces together. May your love be like iron: when it breaks, you can weld the pieces back together.
—*Madagascar (Malagasy)*

A happy man marries the woman he loves; a happier man loves the woman he marries.
*—Africa*

Patience makes a marriage succeed.
*—Ghana (Akan)*

Getting married is nothing: it is assuming the responsibility of marriage that counts.
*—Haiti*

A woman worries about the future until she gets a husband; a man never worries about the future until he gets a wife.
*—Uganda (Ganda)*

He who marries a beauty marries trouble.
*—Nigeria*

Never marry a woman who has bigger feet than you.
*—Mozambique*

If you marry a widow, you have her children as well.
*—Niger, Nigeria (Hausa)*

When a woman enters a marriage, she takes her mother along.
*—Ghana (Akan)*

If a young woman who cannot make soup has a marriage that isn't successful, then it is due to the badness of her soup.
*—Ghana (Akan)*

The food of a wife who speaks sweetly will never be rejected by her husband.
*—Nigeria (Igbo)*

A woman knows when her husband is hungry.
*—Ghana (Akan)*

The stew that the husband does not like shouldn't be prepared by the wife.
*—Nigeria (Yoruba)*

A home is ruined by the husband scolding his wife over food.
*—Kenya (Agikuyu)*

If a marriage is sweet or if it is bitter, it is the one who is married who can tell.
*—Ghana (Akan)*

If a young woman says no to marriage, just wait until her breasts sag.
*—Burundi*

Better fish in the sea than what get caught.
*—Barbados*

Before you marry, keep both eyes open; after marriage, shut one.
*—Jamaica*

The bride in her silliness and inexperience calls marriage "love."
*—Uganda (Ganda)*

A good live-with better than a bad marriage.
*—Barbados*

Marriage got teeth; it bite like crab.
*—Guyana, Jamaica*

Marriage is like a groundnut; you must crack it to see what is inside.
*—Ghana (Akan)*

A bird can be guarded; a wife cannot.  —*East Africa (Kiswahili)*

Marriage isn't like palm wine to be tasted and
spit out.  —*Ghana (Akan)*

One mistake does not warrant the divorce of one's wife.  —*East Africa (Kiswahili)*

A scolding woman has herself to blame when the husband
who liked her puts her away.  —*Angola*

He who does not like chattering women must stay a
bachelor.  —*Congo*

A woman who starts to oppose her husband has found
another place to go.  —*Uganda (Ganda)*

When the treasure house is full, desire ceases.  —*Niger, Nigeria (Hausa)*

Something must be wrong with marriage if God got to
send a priest to bless it.  —*Grenada*

When your wife is a woman of no morals, then she might
as well be someone else's harlot.  —*Ghana (Ashanti)*

You do not keep somebody else's wife.  —*Kenya (Agikuyu)*

What you yearn for makes you throw away what you have.  —*Uganda (Ganda)*

The foolish bird's desire for a few grains makes it enter
the cage and then become trapped.  —*Africa*

An old man who marries a young woman buys a
newspaper for others to read.  —*Brazil*

Husbands are like firewood; if left unattended,
they go out.                                    —*Africa*

Husband is the tie; wife is the parcel: when the tie
breaks, the parcel loosens.                     —*Nigeria (Igbo)*

A child is the girdle of marriage.              —*Malawi*


## ✴ SEX

Where the penis enters, there the child comes out.
                                        —*Burkina Faso (Mamprusi)*

It is easy to have sexual intercourse, but it isn't easy to
give birth.                                     —*Ghana (Akan)*

One who marries for love alone will have bad days
but good nights.                                —*Egypt*

Lovers do not hide their nakedness.             —*Congo*

Love is blind, so you have to feel your way.    —*Brazil*

If you feel her thigh, do not fear her sex.
                                        —*Gambia (Mandinka)*

If a woman loves a man, she will give it to him even
through a hole in a door.                        —*Morocco*

Even if your wife's sex is small, dawn will find you there.
                                        —*Mali (Minyanka)*

The kind woman has a hairless vagina.     —*Burkina Faso (Mamprusi)*

Not all nice houses are good to spend the night in.

—*Gambia (Mandinka)*

He who has sexual intercourse with you habitually
does not cause pain.　　　　　　　　—*Ghana (Akan)*

Better a short penis than sleeping alone.

—*Côte d'Ivoire (Baule)*

A fresh vagina wakes up a weak penis.　　　—*Ghana (Akan)*

A young woman's reputation lies in her buttocks.

—*Ghana (Akan)*

Big buttocks wake up an impotent penis.

—*Ghana (Akan)*

It is the woman who knows the man that calls another
"small penis."　　　　　　　　　　—*Nigeria (Igbo)*

A large penis isn't manhood.　　　　—*Namibia (Ovambo)*

The penis comes erect as if it intends to kill, but the
vagina swallows and tames it.　　　　—*Nigeria (Igbo)*

A laughing penis cannot enter.　　　　　　　—*Liberia*

The vagina has no teeth, but it gradually chews up
the loincloth.　　　　　　　　　　　—*Ghana (Akan)*

If a man withdraws from an uncompleted venture, his
legs become shaky.　　　　　　　　—*Ghana (Akan)*

Readiness is manly.　　　　　　　　—*Ghana (Akan)*

What affects the penis affects the vagina.　　　　—*DRC*

The penis at home never impresses the woman, unless she fucks one outside the home.

—Benin, Nigeria, Togo (Yoruba)

When a man learns night walking, his wife learns to tell lies.

—Africa

If an illicit lover stays around long enough, he may end up as the husband—until the next illicit lover.

—Ethiopia

If you want sex while traveling, travel with your wife.

—Mali (Minyanka)

A woman is attractive when she is somebody else's wife.

—Zimbabwe

No other animal romances the wife of a lion.

—Africa

Many are the eyes of the person whose spouse commits adultery.

—Zambia

Adultery is like dung; one goes far to do it.

—Zambia (Bemba)

A fence does not enter another.

—Burundi

Men and women toward each other are for the eyes and for the heart, and not only for the bed.

—Algeria, Mali, Niger (Tamashek)

## ✳ CLOSENESS AND FAMILIARITY

Love comes from the pillow.                                       —*Lesotho*

The familiar won't be feared.                          —*West Africa (Fulani)*

Once two people have seen each other, they become
known to each other.                                   —*Kenya (Agikuyu)*

He who is familiar to you, if he weeps for you,
weeps profusely.                                        —*Ghana (Akan)*

Wood already touched by fire isn't hard to set alight.
                                                        —*Africa*

What is in the yams that a knife does not know?
                                              —*Sierra Leone (Temne)*

A stone from home is worth ten from the riverbed.
                                              —*North Africa (Berber)*

Birds that drink water at one swamp know each other's
feathers.                                              —*Malawi (Yawo)*

You do not know the extent of waters you haven't
been to.                                       —*Tanzania (Zanzibar)*

You will never drown where you always take a bath.
                                                        —*Mali*

A gunsmith does not fear the mysteries of the forest.
                                       —*Mozambique, Zimbabwe (Shona)*

An everyday path has no signpost.            —*East Africa (Kiswahili)*

He who does not lose his way by night won't lose his way by day.
—*Niger, Nigeria (Hausa)*

Those who live together cannot hide their behinds from each other.
—*Namibia*

Two buttocks cannot avoid brushing.
—*Zambia (Tonga)*

To stay together is to know each other.
—*Kenya (Agikuyu)*

To stay close together isn't a relationship.
—*Malawi (Yawo)*

We cannot dwell in a house together without speaking one to another.
—*Benin, Nigeria, Togo (Yoruba)*

Separation is better than a strained relationship.
—*Kenya (Agikuyu)*

Eggs and iron must not be in the same bag.
—*Sudan*

The panther and the sheep never hunt together.
—*Niger, Nigeria (Hausa)*

The skin fit closer than the shirt.
—*Jamaica*

It takes two to rub each other's backs.
—*East Africa (Kiswahili)*

He who has dust in his eyes cannot blow it off himself.
—*Ghana (Twi)*

The reason two antelope walk together is so that one can blow the dust out of the eyes of the other.
—*Africa*

If a disease affects the nose, the eye is also affected.

—Ghana (Twi)

The monkey's tail is long, and yet if you touch it,
its owner feels the touch.　　　　—Senegal, Gambia (Wolof)

A lizard suns itself within reach of its hiding place.

—Zimbabwe, Mozambique (Shona)

The goat feed where him is tied.　　　　—Jamaica

If you live near the stream, you hear the cough of
the crab.　　　　—Ghana (Twi)

The chicken that is always near the mother gets the thigh
of the grasshopper.　　　　—Ghana

If an animal is biting you, it is from inside your cloth.

—Ghana (Akan)

When a person falls, she becomes acquainted with the
nature of the ground.　　　　—Nigeria (Igbo)

He who remains near the fireplace is the one who puts
out the fire.　　　　—East Africa (Kiswahili)

Excess of familiarity is at the root of all hostility.

—Algeria

If you attach yourself too closely to a human being,
he treats you cheaply.　　　　—Ghana (Akan)

Invite people into your parlor, and they will come into
your bedroom.　　　　—Sierra Leone

A bathing place you are familiar with brings forth a crocodile bite.

—*Zambia (Tonga)*

Play with puppy, puppy lick you mouth.

—*Jamaica*

At home, saints never perform miracles.

—*Brazil*

The camel does not see the bend in its neck.

—*Libya*

People know each other better on a journey.

—*Botswana, South Africa (Tswana)*

It is the hut you know that you go in while it is dark.

—*Burkina Faso (Mamprusi)*

## ❧ HOME

Home is a warm bed for the family. —*South Africa*

A home always has room for the people you love, even if it is crowded. —*Tanzania*

A small house all your own is always big enough. —*Haiti*

The tortoise is the wisest. He carries his own home. —*Mali (Bambara)*

A rat has never lost its hole. —*West Africa (Fulani)*

The frog does not come out of its pool unless it has to. —*South Africa (Zulu)*

A man does not wander far from where his corn is roasting. —*Namibia*

No wanderer can ever know the full meaning of a home. —*Africa*

The journey is never so pleasant that the traveler does not return home. —*Benin, Nigeria, Togo (Yoruba)*

Place value on defending your home. —*Namibia (Ovambo)*

A house of your own is worth wagons of gold. —*South Africa*

Every man is a prince in his own bed. —*Malawi*

Challenge

Aunt Ettie pushed boundaries for as long as I knew her. She allowed no one and nothing to limit her—not color, gender, age, illness, accidents, money, status, or authority. She approached life with the belief that "good fortune will not happen to you; good fortune is given to him who seeks it" (Egypt).

She used her own savings to start a manufacturing business in 1946, during Jamaica's colonial era, when Black men (let alone Black women) found difficulty entering the private sector as employees, let alone owners. Obstacles did not deter her. "Smooth seas do not make skillful sailors" (Namibia)—and her profits allowed her to travel the world for thirty years after she retired in her sixties. She celebrated her eightieth birthday in the Middle East.

Aunt Ettie never married. She would not have called herself a feminist, but she told me she never allowed any man (or woman, for that matter) to manage her life or intimidate her. When she felt convinced I was not finding peace of mind in my marriage, she opened her heart and her checkbook to help me to live alone for the first time in my life. Her example gave me confidence that "there is no hardship that will not end, no trouble that will not retreat" (Namibia).

Three years later, she stood by me again when I decided to give up a corporate job to follow my dream of becoming a writer. She was well aware of the challenge of being an independent Black female, but she showed by example that "one does not forgo sleeping because of the possibility of nightmares" (Niger, Nigeria).

She tackled health crises as if they were temporary detours in her enjoyment of life. Early in her eighties, she recovered from a brain aneurysm with no physical or mental disability. A few years later, a hit-and-run driver left her with a fractured pelvis. Two months after that accident, she was once again living alone in her two-story town house and attending the gym to strengthen her legs, and shortly after that she flew to New York on a winter trip. She credited her physical resilience to good eating: "There is no medicine as active as good food" (Nigeria).

Aunt Ettie made herself happy whether or not she had company. Her good friends, men and women of all ages, valued her as a mentor and counselor. I once asked her if she felt lonely to be in her nineties and losing all her age-mates. She said she had never chained herself to the past: "The olden times are what we see today" (Ghana). Besides, she told me, death happens, and life has to go on. "What comes on your plate is what you swallow" (Uganda).

When she fell ill at ninety-seven, I sensed she had decided to depart with dignity—she never wanted to feel helpless and dependent. I sat at her bedside and told her how much I loved her and how grateful I was for all the lessons she taught me about never being too Black, too female, too old, too ill, or too alone to live life fully. And freely.

## ❋ LUCK AND FORTUNE

Good fortune will not happen to you; good fortune is given to him who seeks it.
—*Egypt*

He who waits for a chance may wait for a long time.
—*Nigeria (Yoruba)*

All head is head, but all luck is not luck.
—*Jamaica*

One man's dead is another one's bread.
—*U.S. Virgin Islands*

The sun don't shine on the same dog's tail all week.
—*United States (Black communities)*

She who laughs on Friday will cry on Sunday.
—*United States (Louisiana Creole)*

If the hare has outwitted the hunters today, tomorrow is still a hunting day.
—*Nigeria (Igbo)*

The tortoise's food is eaten by others. Without quick legs, what can he do?
—*Zambia*

Throw him into the river and he will rise with a fish in his mouth.
—*Africa*

Every day is fishing day, but not every day you catch fish.
—*Jamaica*

Misfortunes do not have set times for coming.
—*Ghana (Twi)*

Misfortune knows no hero.
—*Kenya (Agikuyu)*

Misfortune cannot be rejected with contempt.

*—Kenya (Agikuyu)*

When your luck deserts you, even cold food burns.

*—Zambia*

While running from the rain, you fall into a stream.

*—Haiti*

A windfall will be blown away by the next gust.     *—Africa*

You will meet the cobra when you have no stick.     *—Namibia*

The day you go to hunt, the hare climbs up the trees.

*—Nigeria (Igbo)*

Unlucky lips go through life without a kiss.     *—Ethiopia*

When bad luck hold you, paper itself will cut you.

*—Guyana, Trinidad and Tobago, Barbados*

## ⁂ FEAR

The lion's power lies in our fear of him.     *—Nigeria*

If you are wearing shoes, you do not fear the thorns.

*—Sudan*

One does not forgo sleeping because of the possibility
of nightmares.     *—Niger, Nigeria (Hausa)*

He who is bitten by a snake fears a lizard.

*—Uganda (Ganda)*

Fear to let fall a drop will
always make you spill a lot.

—*Malawi (Wolof)*

If you do not build your
house firmly, you are afraid to
sleep in it.　　　—*Ghana (Twi)*

If you fear the cat, do not
complain if your house is
taken over by rats.　　　—*Africa*

If the panther knew how much
he is feared, he would do
much more harm.　　　—*Burundi*

Where there is nothing to lose, there is nothing to fear.

—*Sudan*

## ❋ ABUSE, HATRED, AND DISLIKE

He who hates, hates himself.　　　　　　—*South Africa (Zulu)*

Hate burns in the preserver.　　　　　　—*East Africa (Kiswahili)*

Hate does not build a house; it dissolves.

—*Namibia (Ovambo)*

Hate people, but do not give them baskets to fetch
water in.　　　　　　—*Trinidad and Tobago*

Hatred does not recognize generosity.　　　—*Ghana (Akan)*

If a bird dislikes you, it shits on you.　　　　　—*Ghana*

The bitter heart eats its owner. *—Central Africa, East Africa,*
*southern Africa (Bantu)*

He who is sweating with hate cannot rule the country.
*—Namibia (Ovambo)*

If someone hates you, he beats your household pet.
*—Ghana (Akan)*

Some men are only strong in their own house—where
they beat their wives. *—Madagascar (Malagasy)*

A slap does not get a woman. *—Burkina Faso (Mamprusi)*

Do not try to make someone hate the person he loves,
for he will still go on loving, but he will hate you.
*—Senegal*

If someone hates you, that need not prevent you from
getting what you want. *—Niger, Nigeria (Hausa)*

Only a fool hates his family. *—Niger, Nigeria (Hausa)*

The medicine for hate is separation. *—West Africa (Fulfulde)*

Love and let the world know; hate in silence.

*—Egypt*

## ❋ ENEMIES AND FOES

There is nobody to whom everybody is an enemy.

—*Kenya (Agîkûyû)*

If you are in the grip of an enemy, you forget to bite.

—*Ghana (Twi)*

He who is surrounded by enemies should learn to sleep with one eye open. —*Africa*

If you have enemies, then travel with your spear. —*Namibia*

If you want to burn down your house, your enemy will lend you a match. —*Zimbabwe*

If your enemy is in trouble, help him. But if he thanks you, do not reply. —*Ghana (Twi)*

Do not whirl a snake in the air when you have killed it; the ones that remain in their holes see you. —*Zimbabwe, South Africa (Tsonga)*

The snake says it does not hate the person who kills it, but the one who calls out, "Look at the snake." —*Martinique*

Do not let your enemies get in the way of your work. —*Niger, Nigeria (Hausa)*

People who fight on the ground should not go up the tree together.

—*Ethiopia, Kenya (Oromo)*

The person who is not on good terms with you shouldn't be sent into the bush to collect herbs for you when you are ill.

—*Ghana (Twi)*

He who loses his enemy weeps not for him.

—*Senegal, Gambia (Wolof)*

When there is no enemy within, the enemies outside cannot hurt you.

—*Africa*

## ❋ FOOLS AND FOOLISHNESS

Everybody loves a fool, but nobody wants him for a son.

—*West Africa (Mandinka)*

When a fool does not succeed in bleaching ebony, he tries to blacken ivory.

—*Ethiopia (Amharic)*

A fool is thirsty in the midst of water.

—*Ethiopia*

A fool and water will go the way they are directed.

—*Ethiopia*

Only a fool believes everything he is told.

—*Ethiopia, Eritrea (Kunama)*

A fool is advised by his enemies.

—*Egypt*

A fool laughs at the spear.

—*Kenya (Agikuyu)*

The foolhardy learn by the flow of blood.

—South Africa (Zulu)

When a fool is cursed, he thinks he is being praised.

—Ethiopia

Any mistake from the wise becomes a new style to a fool.

—Africa

A fool is a wise man's ladder.

—South Africa

It is the fool whose own tomatoes are sold to him.

—Ghana

If you say the chief of your town is stupid, then you yourself are stupid.

—Ghana (Akan)

He who claps his hands for the fool to dance is no better than the fool.

—Benin, Nigeria, Togo (Yoruba)

When a person argues with a fool, the foolish become two.

—Africa

A fool's answer is ever on the edge of his tongue.

—Egypt

One time fool no fool, but two time fool is fool.

—Jamaica

If you put fool in a mortar and beat him and beat him, him come out the same fool.

—Jamaica

A fool at forty is a fool forever.

—Africa

There is no hardship that will not end, no trouble that
will not retreat.
—*Namibia (Ovambo)*

To lose your way is one way of finding it.
—*East Africa (Kiswahili)*

It is crooked wood that shows the best sculptor. —*Africa*

Iron is passed through fire to be hardened.
—*East Africa (Kiswahili)*

Hard living conditions drive sheep and goats to graze in
one pasture.
—*Guyana*

When you are carrying water and happen to spill it, if the
calabash be not broken, you can get more.
—*Benin, Nigeria, Togo*

Not until we have fallen do we know how to rearrange
our burden.
—*Benin, Nigeria, Togo (Yoruba)*

When they strike you on top of your head, they are
strengthening your neck.
—*Ghana (Akan)*

Smooth seas do not make skillful sailors.
—*Namibia (Ovambo)*

Do not look where you fell but where you slipped.
—*Nigeria (Yoruba)*

The horse has four legs but still falls sometimes.
—*South Africa*

Hardship reveals personality.                    —*East Africa (Kiswahili)*

Calamity has no voice; suffering cannot speak to tell who is really in distress.                    —*Benin, Nigeria, Togo (Yoruba)*

Problems do not flap their wings.                    —*Kenya (Agikuyu)*

Trouble does not climb a tree; trouble climbs the person causing it.                    —*Uganda (Ganda, Lugbara)*

It is no good steering clear of trouble yourself if you let another draw you in.                    —*Niger, Nigeria (Hausa)*

Nothing is so difficult that diligence cannot master it.
                    —*Madagascar (Malagasy)*

Our misfortunes are never out of proportion to our capacity to bear them.                    —*Benin, Nigeria, Togo (Yoruba)*

## ⨳ CRITICISM AND COMPLAINT

The fetus that is afraid of criticism is never born.
                    —*Burundi*

What is it that is not criticized?                    —*Uganda (Ganda, Lugbara)*

Those who cannot dance say the music is no good.
                    —*U.S. and British Virgin Islands*

You should not see a person the first time and say to him, "You have lost flesh."                    —*Ghana (Twi)*

"Look at this part of your body! Look at that part of your body!" is not good fellowship.                    —*Ghana (Twi)*

You come here to drink milk, you don't come here to count cow. —*Barbados, Guyana, Jamaica*

Study the reasons for a man's actions before criticizing him. —*Africa*

If you laugh at someone's rough skin, you must be prepared to give him/her oil. —*Kenya (Agikuyu)*

No attention is paid to him who is always complaining. —*Kenya*

Complaining is a weak person's only weapon. —*Africa*

Rheumatism and happiness both get bigger if you keep telling folks about them. —*United States (Black communities)*

Critique does not depreciate the sweetness of honey. —*West Africa*


## ❖ HYPOCRISY

You are always straightening other people's fences; your own are leaning. —*Angola, Namibia (Ovambo)*

Do not mend your neighbor's fence before seeing to your own. —*Tanzania*

A bald man shouldn't tell a closely shaved man that his head is too bare. —*Ghana (Akan)*

If nakedness promises you a dress, first look at what it is wearing. —*Africa*

The hunchback laughs at the one with tremors.

—*South Africa (Zulu)*

A finger does not point at its owner. —*Africa*

Alligator shouldn't call hog "long mouth." —*Jamaica*

Fisherman never say that the fish stink. —*Barbados*

There are those who pass gas in public and then
complain about the smell. —*Ethiopia*

If we are not full grown, we do not laugh at a short man.

—*Ghana (Akan)*

People dislike the frog but drink the water it is in.

—*Ghana (Akan)*

Singing "Alleluia" everywhere does not prove piety.

—*Ethiopia*

He gave a sermon and forgot himself. —*East Africa (Kiswahili)*

He lived with priests and died without being baptized.

—*Haiti*

Beware of the herbalist whose wife sells coffins. —*Africa*

## ⁂ DECEIT AND BETRAYAL

Your neighbor is a snake; she/he kills you without your
knowledge. —*Tanzania*

Not all people who snore are asleep. —*Africa*

All skin-teeth is not laugh. —*Caribbean*

The teeth that laugh are also those that bite. —*West Africa*

The tongue that does buy you does sell you. —*Barbados*

Whispering will be followed by hiding, then stealing.
—*Kenya (Agikuyu)*

The child of deceit is trouble. —*Uganda (Ganda, Lugbara)*

He who betrayed you yesterday will not save you today.
—*Haiti*

Even if Christ's death could have been prevented, Judas
would still be a traitor. —*Ethiopia*

Comrades sometimes betray each other. —*Kenya (Agikuyu)*

No matter how you try to cover up smoke, it must
come out. —*United States (South Carolina Gullah)*

Go away and the conversation changes. —*Malawi*

Back of dog is "dog"; in front of dog is "Mr. Dog."
—*British Virgin Islands, Jamaica, Trinidad and Tobago*

One cannot make a pact with the slave and make a pact
with the master, and then not betray one of them.
—*Benin, Nigeria, Togo (Yoruba)*

If a thousand people are deceiving you to catch you, you
also deceive a thousand in running away from them.
—*Ghana (Twi)*

If the ear does not hear malicious gossip, then the heart
is not grieved. —*Benin, Nigeria, Togo (Yoruba)*

You can't stop you ear from hearing, but you can stop
you mouth from talking. —*Barbados*

Mouth not keeping to mouth, and lip not keeping to lip,
bring trouble to the jaws. —*Benin, Nigeria, Togo (Yoruba)*

Lips break the village. —*Malawi (Yawo)*

Gossip is like a disease; once you have caught it, it is hard
to get rid of. —*East Africa (Kiswahili)*

Like vomit and shit under your feet, the rumormonger
spreads scandal. —*Sudan*

The back of your head has many tongues. —*Africa*

He who chatters with you will chatter about you. —*Egypt*

Friendship ends if there are whisperings.
—*Kenya (Agikuyu)*

Gossiping and lying are brother and sister. —*Kenya*

Often the lips observe things before the eyes do. —*Haiti*

Let us see then tell; hearing is not seeing.
—*Tanzania (Zanzibar)*

The noise of even the loudest events must begin to die
down by the second market week. —*Africa*

The greatest liar is the man who says he never lies.    —*Africa*

A multitude of words cloaks a lie.    —*Niger, Nigeria (Hausa)*

A lie runs until truth overtakes it.    —*Cuba*

Believe the liar up to the door of his house and no further than that.    —*Egypt*

You can lock your door from a thief, but not from a damn liar.    —*U.S. and British Virgin Islands*

If you seek a thing for a thousand years through falsehood, the honest man takes it from your hand in a day.    —*Ghana (Akan)*

One falsehood spoils a thousand truths.    —*Ghana*

When you tell a lie, your insides let you know first.    —*Ethiopia*

When you base what you say on falsehood, you become tired.    —*Ghana (Akan)*

Lying will get you a wife, but it won't keep her.    —*Burundi*

If you start a journey in dishonesty, you get lost.    —*Ghana (Akan)*

The burden of a lie is like a large tin of coals burning fiercely on the head of its carrier.　　　　　*—Mozambique*

An issue starts with two sides, but lying multiplies them.
　　　　　*—Ethiopia*


### ✦ JEALOUSY AND ENVY

Where there is no jealousy, people are able to share the little they have.　　　　　*—Tanzania*

From the well of envy only a fool drinks the water.
　　　　　*—Nigeria*

If a person has, do not let it worry you.　　*—Burkina Faso (Mamprusi)*

Jealousy does not prevent a hardworking person from becoming rich.　　　　　*—Kenya (Agikuyu)*

Jealousy starts from the eye.　　　　　*—South Africa (Zulu)*

Eyes usually envy the ear.　　　　　*—Africa*

Envy is prosperity's manure.　　　　　*—West Africa (Fulani)*

The jealous man loses his flesh by looking at the fat bellies of others.　　　　　*—Congo*

It is not necessary to blow out the other person's lantern to let yours shine.　　　　　*—East Africa (Kiswahili)*

Envy plants an enemy within and becomes self-destructive.　　　　　*—Ethiopia*

A warthog eating its fill does not delight a pig.

—*Mozambique (Sena)*

The jealousy of a wife is the key to her divorce.      —*Egypt*

A stone will sooner soften than jealousy.

—*Botswana, South Africa (Tswana)*

## ⊶ QUARRELS AND CONFLICT

It is the absence of a third person that makes it possible
for two people to fight to the death.

—*Benin, Nigeria, Togo (Yoruba)*

Stop quarrel before fight come.      —*Jamaica*

To fight with everyone can result in a shortage of
pallbearers at your funeral.      —*Ethiopia*

When two elephants fight, it is the grass that suffers.

—*Uganda (Ganda)*

The eyeball and the eyelid shouldn't quarrel.      —*Africa*

A fight does not build the village.      —*Malawi (Yawo)*

He who argues builds no roads.      —*Namibia (Ovambo)*

One who asks, "What did you quarrel about?" renews the
quarrel of yesterday.      —*Uganda (Ganda)*

To quarrel about things that do not belong to you
is to shed tears for nothing.      —*Uganda (Ganda)*

When the border of the land is violated, the center becomes the border. —*Ethiopia*

War or fighting is not food to be eaten. —*Ghana (Twi)*

Do not fight with a toothless man over juicy bones. —*Africa*

Big people do not quarrel over small vegetables, unless they are tasty. —*Uganda (Ganda)*

Do not quarrel over a matter in which you are wrong. —*Egypt*

Do not quarrel with the leopard if you have no spear. —*DRC*

Don't wrestle with hogs. You will both get dirty, and the hog will like it. —*Barbados*

It is over honey that the honeybee becomes aggressive. —*Guinea*

Even Buddhist priests of the same temple quarrel occasionally. —*Senegal*

Even the tongue and the teeth quarrel now and then. —*Nigeria (Nupe)*

Where two quarrel, two are guilty. —*South Africa*

It is on the day when you quarrel that you'll find out the truth. —*Haiti*

When two quarrel, the first to stop is the wisest. —*South Africa*

Two wise men will smile, not quarrel. —*Egypt*

Silence finishes the argument. —*Uganda (Ganda)*

The quiet one puts an end to an argument.
—*Angola, Namibia (Ovambo)*

Avoiding a quarrel is better than asking forgiveness.
—*Niger, Nigeria (Hausa)*

## ❈ ANGER

The warrior fights with courage, not with anger.
—*Ghana (Twi)*

Getting angry brings loss. —*Kenya (Agikuyu)*

In anger, there is no intelligence. —*Tanzania (Sukuma)*

Anger's brother is dissension. —*Ghana (Akan)*

Anger and madness are brothers. —*Africa*

Anger is like a wanderer; it does not live in one
man's house. —*Ghana (Twi)*

Anger drives something good from the house.
—*Ghana (Akan)*

It is better to walk fast than to grow angry at the forest.
—*Senegal*

Bad temper kills its owner. —*Ghana (Twi)*

As the wound inflames the finger, so the thought
inflames the mind. —*Ethiopia*

As long as fire stays in one's breast, it does not
cool down. —*Ethiopia*

Anger brings with it a long tale. —*Ghana (Akan)*

A stone thrown in anger never kills a bird.
—*Nigeria (Yoruba)*

Anger without power is a ready blow. —*Egypt*

If you hold your anger, it will kill all your happiness.
—*United States (South Carolina Gullah)*

To spend the night in anger is better than to spend
it in repentance. —*Senegal*

A mother's wrath does not survive the night. —*Burundi*

To get rid of anger, first weed out the bitter roots.
—*Zambia*

The greatest remedy for anger is delay. —*East Africa (Kiswahili)*

## ✳ FORGIVENESS

He who forgives gains the victory in the dispute.
—*Nigeria (Yoruba)*

If you do not forgive a crime, you commit a crime.
—*Ghana (Twi)*

He who does not know how to forgive, let him not expect
to be forgiven. —*East Africa (Kiswahili)*

If you offend, ask for pardon; if offended, forgive.
—*Ethiopia*

You cannot throw away you finger because it hurt you.
—*Guyana*

If God were not forgiving, heaven would be empty.
—*North Africa (Berber)*

Can the ant forget that the elephant stepped on him?
—*Kenya*

It is easier to forgive than to forget. —*South Africa*

All errors are amendable. —*Africa*

## ❈ SADNESS AND SORROW

If we say we do not weep, this does not apply to widows.
—*Ghana (Akan)*

Even a clever woman can settle nothing the day her
husband dies. —*Mali (Minyanka)*

One weeps for his own mother at the funeral of
someone else's mother. —*Ghana*

To weep does not ease the heart. —*Botswana, South Africa (Tswana)*

Crying a lot does not give you peace of mind. —*Burundi*

It is not all tears that show sadness.  —*Ghana (Akan)*

Any kind of crying will do for a funeral.

—*United States (North Carolina)*

They who weep cannot weep beyond the cemetery.

—*Ghana (Akan)*

The gravediggers
forget quickly, but
the bereaved don't.
—*Tanzania (Sukuma)*

You cannot cry
louder than the
bereaved.

—*Africa*

The tears in your
eyes do not blind
you.  —*Togo*

Nothing dries faster than tears.  —*Haiti*

Many days of laughter are wiped away by one moment
of mourning.  —*Uganda (Ganda)*

No one who is gloomy should stay in the dark.  —*Ghana (Akan)*

I've been in sorrow's kitchen and licked out all the pots.

—*United States (South Carolina Gullah)*

The stiff breeze bends the bush in whichever direction
it pleases; the person in control may send one
wherever he or she wishes.          —*Benin, Nigeria, Togo (Yoruba)*

He who has no power depends on the one who has.
          —*Ghana*

The train does not wait for the passenger.
          —*Mozambique (Tsonga)*

When the lion roars, all the animals are quiet.
          —*East Africa (Kiswahili)*

A thing that cannot speak obeys the one who can.
          —*Uganda (Ganda)*

If the bird can scream, it cannot be caught by the
wild beast.          —*Ghana (Twi)*

The elephant does not take flight at the sight of a dog.
Even the owner of two hundred dogs cannot chase
an elephant.          —*Benin, Nigeria, Togo (Yoruba)*

Even if cockroaches come in thousands, one chicken
can clear them all.          —*Nigeria (Igbo)*

The lion does not fear the dog, but its master.          —*Sudan*

Butter cannot fight against the sun.          —*Uganda (Ganda)*

Every power is subject to another power.
          —*Mozambique, Zimbabwe (Shona)*

Fire can soften iron. —DRC (Nkundo-Mongo)

Even an ant can hurt an elephant. —South Africa (Zulu)

The lord of the elephant is the sun. —Uganda (Ganda, Lugbara)

A flea can trouble a lion more than the lion can
harm a flea. —Kenya

O wind, you have no weight, but you cut down the
biggest trees. —Niger, Nigeria (Hausa)

Authority does not depend on age. —Namibia (Ovambo)

Even an old woman runs on God's errands. —Kenya (Oromo)

Where there is power, there is no opposition. —Ghana (Akan)


## ⠶ STRENGTH

The strong do not need clubs. —Senegal

One blow will not knock a strong man down.
—Niger, Nigeria (Hausa)

A strong man beats you with the stick that you had in
your own hands. —Uganda (Ganda)

If you fail to take away a strong man's sword when he
is on the ground, will you do it when he gets up?
—Nigeria

He who torments another only teaches him to
strengthen himself. —Benin, Nigeria, Togo (Yoruba)

Rain does not kill the strength of hot pepper.

—*Haiti*

Even if you are strong, you are not stronger than a stone.

—*Ghana (Akan)*

A stone is never overturned by the wind.

—*DRC (Mongo)*

To tame a spirit, you have to be a stronger spirit.

—*Zimbabwe*

The strength of the crocodile is the water.

—*Africa*

Guile excels strength.

—*Niger, Nigeria (Hausa)*

Hurrying and worrying are not the same as strength.

—*Niger, Nigeria (Hausa)*

## ❀ CAUTION AND SAFETY

If you do not use Saturday to keep watch on the road, you will use Sunday to run away.

—*Ghana (Twi)*

He who guards himself will not perish.

—*Namibia (Ovambo)*

Take care more better nor be sorry.

—*United States (South Carolina Gullah)*

A dog cannot bite you when it has warned you.　　　—Burundi

If you hear the bridge cracking, get out of the way.
　　　　　　　　　　　　　　　　　　　—Jamaica

Go round the long way, and arrive in safety.　　—Uganda (Ganda)

If there are crocodiles in the water, take your bath in
a gourd.　　　　　　　　　　　　　—Niger, Nigeria (Hausa)

No one tests the depth of the river with both feet.
　　　　　　　　　　　　　　　　　　　　—Ghana

If you catch a crab, you hold its claws.　　　　—Ghana (Akan)

Hot needle burn thread.　　　　　　　　　　　—Jamaica

A bearded man shouldn't blow on fire.　　　　　—Africa

Put out the fire while it is small.　　　　—Niger, Nigeria (Hausa)

It is a low fire that warms the soup.
　　　　　　　　　　　　—Zimbabwe, Mozambique (Shona)

A distant fire does not burn.　　　　—East Africa (Kiswahili)

A delicate thing is not difficult to injure.
　　　　　　　　　　　　　　　—Benin, Nigeria, Togo (Yoruba)

The butterfly that brushes against thorns will
tear its wings.　　　　　　　　—Benin, Nigeria, Togo (Yoruba)

The rose petals fall, but the thorns remain.　　　—Haiti

Until a rotten tooth is removed, one must
chew carefully.　　　　　　　　　　　　　　　—Nigeria

The fact that a housefly has entered the mouth does not mean that it should be allowed to enter the stomach.

*—Africa*

The mosquito says grace too loud for his own good before getting ready to eat. *—United States (Black communities)*

Ants die in sugar. *—Malawi*

Bee that have honey in the mouth have poison in the tail.

*—Belize*

Honey is the daughter of the bee. *—Uganda (Ganda, Lugbara)*

The protected person is often unaware of reality.

*—Suriname*

Do not talk about a rhinoceros if there is no tree nearby.

*—South Africa (Zulu)*

You do not look upward at a tree that you know you are not supposed to climb. *—Burundi*

When you hold the ground, you cannot fall.

*—Nigeria (Annang)*

The man whose skill in throwing a spear is known; you do not wait till he brandishes it at you. *—Uganda (Ganda)*

When you throw your spear at an elephant, make sure you do not miss. *—Liberia*

One can wield a knife only where an elephant is already dead. Who dares do so in the presence of a living elephant? *—Benin, Nigeria, Togo (Yoruba)*

If there is nothing anywhere, then we wouldn't close
the door when we sleep.                           —Ghana (Akan)

Never open any door you cannot close.            —Barbados


## ❈ READINESS, PLANNING, AND
   PREPARATION

Readiness has no fears.                            —Ghana (Twi)

When the mouse laughs at the cat, there is a hole nearby.
                                    —Senegal, Gambia (Wolof)

When a blind man threaten to stone you, he probably
have the stone secure under he foot.             —Guyana

A woman's rope is ready on the porch.       —Uganda (Ganda)

A snake always leaves home with its poison.       —Africa

What you recognize as deadly will not kill you.
                                             —Uganda (Ganda)

If you go dance with crocodile, you better plan what
you going to do when dance done.                  —Guyana

One who asks for mashed food has someone to mash
it for him/her.                              —Kenya (Agikuyu)

Keep your eyes open even when your teeth fall out.
                                                  —Namibia

An army without good planning is conquered with
one club.                                    —Kenya (Agikuyu)

He who provokes a war must be sure that he knows
how to fight.
—*Mozambique (Tsonga)*

Because of the arrow, we make the shield.
—*Ghana (Akan)*

Carry a weapon always; one day
it will be useful to you.
—*East Africa (Kiswahili)*

A person does not begin to
forge a gun when the war
has already arrived in the
village.
—*Malawi (Nyanja)*

You do not start to make a
shield on the battlefield.
—*Ghana (Twi)*

Before shooting, one must
aim.
—*Senegal, Gambia (Wolof)*

Before one cooks, one must have the meat.
—*Mauritania*

If a man wants to be friendly with wolves, he must
first sharpen his spear.
—*Zimbabwe*

You have not yet obtained the loaf, and you begin to
prepare your stew?
—*Benin, Nigeria, Togo (Yoruba)*

You measure the animal's neck and then you tie him up.
—*Ghana*

When you buy a cow at the market, do not forget to buy
a rope as well.
—*Africa*

Who don't have knife can't eat pineapple.
—*Jamaica*

Do not measure the timbers for your house in the forest.

*—Liberia*

You cannot build a house for last year's summer.

*—Ethiopia*

Any fool destroying the bridge linking his village to the mainland must be sure that he knows how to swim.

*—Africa*

Prepare yourself for when the water comes up to your knees.

*—Congo*

When you think of running, think also about getting tired.

*—Haiti*

One does not start building a fire when the wind blows hard.

*—Ethiopia*

The day you are leaving is not the time to start your preparations.

*—Nigeria*

If you want to make love, first look for a mat.

*—Côte d'Ivoire (Baule)*

Caution is not cowardice; even ants march armed.

*—Uganda (Ganda)*

For the sake of the future, a person grows nails.

*—Ghana (Akan)*

When one is prepared, difficulties do not come.

*—Ethiopia*

Walk with a stick when the person ahead of you slips.

*—East Africa (Kiswahili)*

The stick cannot be called when needed. —*Tanzania (Sukuma)*

You can only jump over a ditch if you have seen it
from afar. —*Africa*

To make preparations does not spoil the trip. —*Guinea*

Do not enter without knowing your exit beforehand.
—*Ethiopia*

## ✳ PRIORITY AND FOCUS

In the larger affairs, the minor are forgotten. —*Angola*

A fugitive never stops to pick thorns from his feet.
—*Africa*

If your part of the battlefield is covered with thorns,
you do not leave your position and go to stand where
the ground is good. —*Ghana (Twi)*

Two men in a burning house must not stop to argue.
—*Cameroon*

Save your relative from trouble before chiding him
for having caused the trouble. —*Nigeria (Igbo)*

Pull the child out of the water before you
punish him/her. —*Liberia, Sierra Leone (Vai)*

The hen with baby chicks does not swallow the worm.
—*Sudan*

Someone does not leave the death of a child to go and
involve herself in quarrels of fellow wives. —*Ghana (Akan)*

When your eyes are poked, your grip on someone's throat loosens.
*—Ethiopia*

If you do not even find time to make a door for your doorway, it will take you three years to find your property.
*—Ghana (Akan)*

He who has been invited to eat meat does not waste time looking for good clothes to wear.
*—Kenya (Agikuyu)*

Fry the big fish first, the little one after.
*—Jamaica*

You do not have to turn and look at every dog that barks.
*—Haiti*

If your horse can race well, you do not use it to run after birds.
*—Ghana (Dagbani)*

The hunter in pursuit of an elephant does not stop to throw stones at birds.
*—Uganda (Ganda)*

The noise of the river drowns the noise of the people.
*—Benin, Nigeria, Togo (Yoruba)*

If you are building a house and a nail breaks, do you stop building, or do you change the nail?
*—Rwanda*

Do not let what you cannot do tear from your hands what you can.
*—Ghana (Ashanti)*

One who enters a forest does not listen to the breaking of the twigs in the brush.
*—Zambia*

When you are asked to look up, never lose sight of what is on the ground.
*—Africa*

## ❋ MODERATION

A cow is milked by gentle hands. — *Niger, Nigeria (Hausa)*

"Give me a push from my back" does not mean "give me a hunchback." — *Nigeria*

A bow that is stretched to the limit breaks. — *Zambia (Bemba)*

A trap whose string is too stiff lets the bird escape. — *Ghana*

Being involved in conspiracy can backfire; too much sharpening of the knife can result in cutting oneself. — *Ethiopia*

A house should not be built so close to another that a chicken from one can lay an egg in the neighbor's yard, nor so far away that a child cannot shout to the yard of his neighbor. — *Tanzania*

If you go to fireside and see food, eat half and leave half. — *Jamaica*

When belly full, jaw must stop. — *Jamaica*

He steals a little, it is overlooked, and then he steals much. — *Angola, Namibia (Ovambo)*

If the stream is not checked, it will cross the road. — *Ghana (Twi)*

If all seeds that fall were to grow, then no one could follow the path under the trees. — *Nigeria*

There is no one who became rich because he broke
a holiday and no one who became fat because he broke
a fast. —*Ethiopia*

To be hard does not mean to be hard as a stone, and to
be soft does not mean to be soft as water. —*Kenya (Agikuyu)*

## ⋇ ORDER AND PROCESS

We count one before we count two. —*Ghana (Akan)*

A woman who wants to have a child must raise her
front apron. —*Kenya (Agikuyu)*

The belly precedes the child. —*Burundi (Rundi)*

A child is never old before its parents. —*East Africa (Kiswahili)*

Before you walk you have to creep. —*Jamaica*

Heel never go before toe. —*Jamaica*

No matter how much you turn around, your heels
will always be behind you. —*Nigeria (Igbo)*

For a bird to know how to fly, it must first learn
how to leave its nest. —*Zambia*

No one completes a journey and then goes back
to look for the beginning. —*Ghana (Akan)*

Before the beard was born, the eyebrow was
already living. —*Ghana (Akan)*

Before eating, open your mouth. —*Mauritania*

Do not swallow before you chew.
—*Zimbabwe, Mozambique (Shona), Madagascar*

The ceiling is swept before the floor. —*Ghana*

When one would climb a tree, one begins from the
bottom and not from the top. —*Ghana (Ashanti)*

See the candle light before you blow out the match.
—*Jamaica*

The point of the needle must pass first. —*Ethiopia*

The thread shall always follow the needle. —*Africa*

If it thunders, wait for the rain. —*Malawi (Yawo)*

No rain, no rainbow. —*Jamaica*

Little by little grow the bananas. —*Congo, Tanzania*

A little shrub may grow into a tree. —*Sudan*

Height is not to be hurried. —*Zimbabwe (Ndebele)*

The moon moves slowly, but it gets across the town.
—*Ghana*

One day cannot make an elephant rot. —*Zambia (Lozi)*

A changed place cannot transform an individual,
but a transformed individual can change a place. —*Africa*

The last buffalo has blood on its tail. —*Uganda (Ganda, Lugbara)*

The place we pass through in going we pass through in
returning.
*—Ghana (Akan)*

Night is followed by day, famine by abundance.
*—Angola, Namibia (Ovambo)*

Sunrise is necessarily followed by sunset. *—Kenya (Agikuyu)*

Today cannot catch tomorrow. *—Africa*

Today is the elder brother of tomorrow, and copious dew
is the elder brother of rain. *—Benin, Nigeria, Togo (Yoruba)*

All things have their time and an end. *—Ghana (Twi)*


## ⟫⟫ EARTH AND LAND

We are at peace as long as our children are with us and
our land is under our control. *—Ethiopia*

As long as we are in our land, bread is like steak.
*—Ethiopia*

The earth provides for those who nourish it.
*—Benin, Nigeria, Togo (Yoruba)*

If the earth does not give birth to grass and grain, we die.
*—Sudan*

The soil said to a man, "Bring me your seed, not
your need." *—Eritrea*

You cannot deprive the earth of possessions. *—Kenya (Agikuyu)*

The earth opens its mouth for all.     *—Uganda (Ganda, Lugbara)*

The earth is a beehive; we all enter by the same door.

*—Africa*

The earth does not abhor a corpse.     *—Ghana (Akan)*

Whatever is above must come to earth.     *—Ghana (Akan)*

The earth does not grow fat.     *—South Africa (Zulu)*

We have not inherited this land from our ancestors;
rather, we have borrowed it from our children.     *—Kenya*

## ⊰⊱ APPROPRIATENESS

Blow your horn in a herd of elephants; crow in the
company of cockerels; bleat in a flock of goats.     *—Malawi*

Cockroach ain't got no right at hen party.     *—Barbados*

The country rooster does not crow in town.

*—East Africa (Kiswahili)*

A lobster loves water, but not when he's being cooked
in it.     *—Senegal*

You can't take popgun to kill alligator.     *—Jamaica*

Do not plant a seed in the sea.     *—East Africa (Kiswahili)*

Cut pumpkin cannot keep.     *—Barbados*

Do not use an ax to do embroidery.     *—Malawi*

Do not tell any more fairy tales when the child has
gone to sleep.
*—Burundi*

"I won't tie up the mule in a horse's place," says
the widow.
*—North Africa (Berber)*

A man builds the top of his door entrance according
to his height.
*—Ethiopia*

A big fish is caught with big bait.
*—Sierra Leone*

Ackee love fat and okra love salt.
*—Jamaica*

He who has no spoon will burn his hands.
*—Mauritania*

What fits into the mouth gives you a chance to chew
it properly.
*—Uganda (Ganda)*

You cannot chew bone with gum.
*—Barbados*

Eat coconuts while you have teeth.
*—Senegal*

Eat when the meal is ready; speak when the time is ripe.
*—Ethiopia*

If a child is cutting a piece of yam, he cuts it according
to the size of his mouth.
*—Ghana (Twi)*

The gun that we go to war with and drive away the
enemies we do not use in child's play.
*—Ghana (Akan)*

If the drum has a head, it shouldn't be beaten at
the sides.
*—Ghana (Twi)*

If the road is long, you shorten it with your feet, not
with an ax.
*—Ghana*

When the music changes, so does the dance.

—Niger, Nigeria (Hausa)

Move your neck according to the music.   —Ethiopia, Kenya (Oromo)

It is not every field that is suitable for cultivation.   —Africa

When the vine entwines your roof, it is time to cut
it down.

—Cameroon

You in the right church but in the wrong pew.   —Jamaica

The place to wait for a boat is near the river.

—Gambia (Mandinka)

The stream knows where to flow.   —Tanzania (Kuria)

Big ship need deep water.   —Jamaica

There are three things that if one does not know,
one cannot live long in the world: what is too much
for one, what is too little for one, and what is just
right for one.

—East Africa (Kiswahili)

## ⽊ ACCEPTANCE

Some things in life are such that you cannot swallow
them and you cannot spit them.   —Ethiopia

What comes on your plate is what you swallow.

—Uganda (Ganda)

Those who work during the night shouldn't blame the
moon for disturbing them.   —Benin, Nigeria, Togo (Yoruba)

Once you make up your mind to cross a river by walking through, you do not complain of getting your stomach wet.

*—Ghana, Togo (Ewe)*

One who bathes willingly with cold water does not feel the cold.

*—Tanzania*

When the monkey reigns, dance before him.

*—Egypt*

He who sends another to consult a medicine man on his behalf will have to accept whatever advice is given.

*—Kenya (Agikuyu)*

If you cannot stop your father's home from being looted, you might as well join the fray and salvage something.

*—Ethiopia*

If death has come and killed your father and your mother, do not weep saying, "My father and my mother are dead," but weep and say, "I and my father and my mother will go with you."

*—Ghana (Ashanti)*

Those who want rain must also accept the mud.

*—Africa*

Accept the weather as it comes and people as they are.

*—Haiti*

## OPPORTUNITY

Once the lid is off the honey jar, anyone can eat her fill.

*—Madagascar (Malagasy)*

A fallen tree attracts many axes.

*—Ethiopia*

The mouth that does not eat is an invitation to the
mouth that does eat. —*South Africa (Sotho)*

The man on his feet carries off the share of the man
sitting down. —*Guinea*

The elephant is stabbed by all before it falls.
—*South Africa (Zulu)*

The best time to buy children from insane people is
when they sell them. —*Gambia (Mandinka)*

The opportunity that God sends does not wake up
him who is asleep. —*Senegal*

## ⚹ ABILITY

A basket cannot hold water. —*Africa*

That which leaks cannot stay full. —*Namibia*

You cannot cross the ocean by swimming.
—*East Africa (Kiswahili)*

A stick that is out of reach cannot help you in your fight.
—*Mozambique (Tsonga)*

Skill is stronger than strength. —*Africa*

Although the snake does not fly, it has caught the
bird whose home is in the sky. —*Ghana (Akan)*

Gather firewood to the capacity of the string.
—*South Africa (Zulu)*

Do not make your weight heavy when your balance
is weak.
                                                    —*Egypt*

Had I not seen him carrying it, I should have said that
he was unable to.
                                        —*Niger, Nigeria (Hausa)*

Every back is fitted to the burden.
                            —*United States (South Carolina Gullah)*

You cannot stretch your hands further than the bones
in them will allow.
                                                —*Cameroon*

If you can walk, you can dance; if you can talk, you
can sing.
                                                —*Zimbabwe*

She who is naturally gifted in anything becomes expert
in it.
                                        —*Niger, Nigeria (Hausa)*

The ability to dance is inherent in a lame person;
it is the legs that are the handicap.       —*Benin, Nigeria, Togo (Yoruba)*

If we put a hammer in every person's hand, could they
all become blacksmiths?
                                                —*Ghana*

The wind and the imagination can travel far and wide
at no cost.
                                                —*Ethiopia*

One cannot both feast and become rich.
                                                —*Africa*

Common sense is enough; leave wisdom to kings.

*—Malawi*

Common sense born before book.  *—Barbados, Grenada, Tobago*

What is sensible today may be madness another time.

*—Nigeria (Yoruba)*

If boat don't have good bottom, it stay near the shore.

*—Jamaica*

Never make you sail too big for you ship.  *—Jamaica*

If you are hiding, do not light a fire.  *—Ghana*

If you are going to cut a hornet's nest with your hand
and someone offers you a stick, you shouldn't say it is
too short.  *—Ghana (Twi)*

You should never rub butts with a porcupine.  *—West Africa*

An animal with a long tail should not attempt to jump
over a bonfire.  *—Africa*

One who sees the tortoise in tears needn't ask it if all
is well.  *—Nigeria (Igbo)*

The toad likes water, but not when it is boiling.  *—Guinea*

If you trample on a blind man's testicles, next time he
hears your footsteps, he will close his legs.

*—Gambia (Mandinka)*

A leaky house can fool the sun, but it cannot fool
the rain.

—*Haiti*

Ev'ry grin-teet' don' mean laugh.

—*United States (South Carolina Gullah)*

Every shut eye do not mean sleep.

—*United States (South Carolina Gullah)*

You can't stand far away and throw salt in the pot.

—*Jamaica*

You cannot tie a knot without using your thumb.

—*Ghana (Twi)*

You do not ask for palm oil with a gourd that has
no opening.

—*Ghana (Twi)*

You see somebody on top of the palm tree and ask
whether he is healthy or not; if he is not in good health,
could he have climbed the palm tree?

—*Benin, Nigeria, Togo (Yoruba)*

You do not break the calabash from which you
drink wine.

—*Ghana (Twi)*

One does not blow the fire with water in the mouth.

—*Kenya (Agikuyu)*

Do not tie up a dog with a chain of sausages.

—*United States (Louisiana Creole)*

Sickness is like rain; it falls on every roof.          —*Africa*

When suffering knocks at your door and you tell him
there is no seat left for him, he tells you not to worry
because he has brought his own stool.          —*Africa*

For a rash to heal, you must stop scratching.

—*Tanzania (Sukuma)*

There is no cure for him who hides an illness.          —*Ethiopia*

To know the disease is half the cure.          —*Africa*

If you do not have to attend to your illness, then
you have time to die.          —*Ghana (Akan, Twi)*

Medicine left in the bottle cannot help.          —*West Afrika (Yoruba)*

If the dose of medicine tastes nasty, swallow it fast.

—*Grenada, Tobago*

The thorn in your foot is temporarily appeased, but
it is still in.          —*United States (South Carolina Gullah)*

There is no medicine as active as good food.          —*Nigeria (Igbo)*

A diseased village is a good village to a medicine man.

—*Africa*

A good herbalist does not need to advertise himself.

—*Africa*

Good health is worth all your money.          —*South Africa*

Suffer or pay the medicine man.          —*DRC*

The physician's fee is not paid till the sickness is over.
          —*Ghana (Ashanti)*

They have cured my swollen testicles, but they have also
cut them off!          —*Uganda (Ganda)*

A person who has something the matter with him sits
near the fire even when the sun is hot.          —*Kenya (Agikuyu)*

Man can do as much as he like, but not for as long as
he like.          —*Guyana*

One with a scar, do not think him healed.
          —*Tanzania (Zanzibar)*

Visitors' footfalls are like medicine; they heal the sick.
          —*Central Africa, East Africa, southern Africa (Bantu)*

A healthy ear can stand hearing sick words.          —*Senegal*

Before healing others, heal yourself.          —*Gambia*

Health is a crown, and no one knows it save a sick
person.          —*East Africa (Kiswahili)*

## ✳ TIME

The day after tomorrow belongs to the fool.  —*Kenya (Agikuyu)*

To have time is to waste time.  —*Uganda (Ganda)*

Delay is the destruction of work.  —*Niger, Nigeria (Hausa)*

Much is gained if time is gained.  —*South Africa*

Dawn does not come twice to awaken anyone.
—*South Africa (Xhosa)*

Moon does run till day catch it.  —*Trinidad and Tobago*

When the sun shines, bask in it before it is too late.
—*Malawi (Yawo)*

No wait to get there tomorrow; take time get there today.
—*Jamaica*

Tomorrow is pregnant; who knows what it will deliver?
—*Nigeria (Igbo)*

In time, "twenty years" becomes tomorrow.
—*Benin, Nigeria, Togo (Yoruba)*

Nothing don't happen before its time.
—*Barbados, Guyana, Trinidad and Tobago, Jamaica*

Little boy can't climb ladder to turn big man.  —*Barbados*

No man wins against time.  —*South Africa*

Even though the old man is strong and hearty, he will not live forever. —*Ghana*

Even the best boat will one day sink. —*Mali (Bambara)*

Better to start in time than to hurry when it is too late. —*Africa*

Is not the same day leaf fall in water that it rot. —*Jamaica*

You do not start clearing the bush for a new farm and finish the same day. —*Ghana (Twi)*

What don't happen in a year happen in a day. —*Barbados, Guyana, Jamaica*

Time causes remembrance. —*Nigeria (Efik)*

The olden times are what we see today. —*Ghana (Twi)*

Time longer than rope. —*Jamaica*

Be sure to be on the dance place before the drum begins. —*Uganda (Ganda)*

Ethics
and
Values

Everyone—family, friends, farm employees, villagers, and strangers—called my grandmother "Miss Annie." She attended church, sang in the choir, played the church organ, and taught Sunday school all her life. However, her God was not locked into Sunday worship and did not confine himself to a place above the skies. Her God and his agents, her ancestors, were with her day and night all seven days of the week, because "he who makes calculations without God will calculate forever" (Ethiopia).

As a child, I considered Miss Annie's woodstove an altar, a center of nurturing and healing. Her God and her ancestors guided her to recipes for inventive meals and for herbal remedies that nourished and healed mind, body, and spirit. She was in her kitchen by about four each morning, preparing breakfasts that could include cornmeal porridge, liver and onions, fried johnnycakes, and boiled green bananas. She routinely cooked enough to feed at least ten extra mouths. Then, when her visitors were leaving with a full stomach, she offered them gifts (more food, or even advice) to take away. When she was bedridden with a stroke, she would insist that any visitor to the farm must be fed and presented with even an orange or a bag of tamarinds from the farm. She showed that "giving is a matter of the heart; do not say it is a matter of wealth" (East Africa).

She always had the free labor she needed when the time came for her to set up her kitchen garden. Men from the nearby village helped to plough the land, sow the seeds, and tend to the seedlings. During the year, they would share with Miss Annie any crops she did not grow on the farm. In turn, Miss Annie would supply farm workers with daily meals and gifts of garden produce. Their wives had milk free from the farm, especially if they were pregnant or lactating, and their children would be fed whenever they visited my grandmother. Her life seemed the epitome of the Ghanaian proverb "Kindness allows a person to eat food he did not buy."

Miss Annie never seemed cross when her children or grandchildren misbehaved, and she never spanked a child. Instead, she would tell a story with a moral, set a scripture verse to be learned by heart, or use an apt proverb to remind those in error of the values from which they had departed. She believed that "truth keeps the hand cleaner than soap" (Ghana).

Today, more than three decades since Miss Annie's death, her stories and proverbs surface in response to need. "A child asked her mother to teach her proverbs. Her mother told her that a thing must happen to necessitate a proverb" (Nigeria). I feel my grandmother's presence in my kitchen when I feed others or when I create meals that remind me of the smells from her kitchen. Most of all, her words and actions return to me as a guide through difficult times. I am never in doubt that, according to a proverb from Cameroon, "richness of spirit and heart begets richness of cloth and coin."

## ✳ GOD

God made the sea, we make the ship; He made the wind, we make the sail; He made the calm, we make oars.

*—Africa*

Man looks only on the outside of things; God looks into the very heart.

*—Nigeria (Efik)*

No one can uproot the tree that God planted. *—Nigeria (Yoruba)*

No one has to teach a child that God exists.

*—Ghana (Twi)*

God's witness is conscience.

*—Ghana (Akan)*

Lying face upward, I do not see God. How could you see God lying face downward?

*—Ghana (Twi)*

Acts of God are like riddles.

*—Burundi (Rundi)*

God speaks a foreign tongue.

*—Namibia (Ovambo)*

Where God cooks, there is no smoke.

*—Zambia*

If you flee from God, you are still under God.

*—Ghana (Akan)*

If God breaks your leg, He will teach you how to limp.

*—Ghana (Dagbani)*

If God gives you a cup of wine and an evil-minded person kicks it over, He fills it up again.

*—Ghana (Twi)*

When an enemy digs a grave for you, God gives you an emergency exit.
—*Burundi (Kirundi)*

God gives nothing to those who keep their arms crossed.
—*Mali (Bambara)*

God has only one measure for all people.
—*Haiti*

God is the blacksmith who does not forge for only one.
—*Zambia (Bemba)*

What God has foreordained no human being can change.
—*Ghana (Twi)*

God don't always come, but He does send.
—*Grenada, Guyana*

If it is God who sends you, He'll pay your expenses.
—*Haiti*

A mortal owns the saying, and God owns the fulfillment.
—*Burkina Faso (Mamprusi)*

He who makes calculations without God will calculate forever.
—*Ethiopia*

When the day has not yet ended, you do not grumble against God.
—*Ghana (Akan)*

When you stand with the blessing of your mother and God, it matters not who stands against you.
—*Benin, Nigeria, Togo (Yoruba)*

God will help you if you get up.
—*Nigeria (Efik)*

## ❋ PURPOSE AND DESTINY

Fate makes a man dismount quicker than counsel.

—*Niger, Nigeria (Hausa)*

No one collects someone else's destiny.    —*Ghana (Akan)*

What's destined to be yours no one can take away
from you.    —*Haiti*

Run as hard as a wild beast if you will, but you won't get
any reward greater than that destined for you.    —*Egypt*

The tree usually falls in the direction it leans.    —*Africa*

When coconut fall from tree, it cannot fasten back.

—*Barbados*

In the end, a man is alone with his fate.    —*East Africa (Kiswahili)*


## ❋ PRAYER, FAITH, AND HOPE

Everything is formed by habit, even praying.    —*Egypt*

Pray for life, not for money.    —*Ghana (Akan)*

Anticipate the good, so that you may enjoy it.    —*Ethiopia*

Hope makes a good breakfast but a bad supper.    —*Nigeria*

What one hopes for is always better than what one has.

—*Ethiopia*

He who waits for a dead man's shoe will go barefoot
a long time.                                               *—Africa*

The unlucky man's hope prevented him from
committing suicide.                                        *—Burundi*

The darkness of night cannot stop the light of morning.
                                                          *—Burundi*

You do not give up to despair before God.                 *—Burundi*


## ❋ TRUTH

Truth and morning become light with time.        *—Côte D'Ivoire*

The truth is like gold: keep it locked up and you will find
it exactly as you first put it away.                      *—Senegal*

Truth is like sugar cane: even if you chew it for a long
time, it is still sweet.                        *—Madagascar (Malagasy)*

If you use truth in settling a matter, it settles easily.
                                                          *—Africa*

A story got three sides—the right, the wrong, and the
truth.                                                    *—Guyana*

He who leaves truth behind returns to it.
                                            *—East Africa (Kiswahili)*

The one who is defeated through truth does not come
back.                                           *—Kenya (Agikuyu)*

If you are speaking the truth, we do not say your speech is too long.

*—Ghana (Akan)*

Every man know where him own house leak.

*—Belize, U.S. and British Virgin Islands, Jamaica*

One does not leave truthfulness inside to purchase wickedness on credit.

*—Benin, Nigeria, Togo (Yoruba)*

Truth came to market but could not be sold; however, we buy lies with ready cash.

*—Ghana (Ashanti)*

Bitter truth is better than sweet falsehood.

*—East Africa (Kiswahili)*

Do not swear that you'll always speak the truth, just speak it.

*—Uganda (Ganda)*

The speaker of truth has no friends.

*—East Africa (Kiswahili)*

Truth is not afraid of the gun.

*—Ghana (Akan)*

The truth passes through fire and does not burn.

*—Burundi (Rundi)*

Truth keeps the hand cleaner than soap.

*—Ghana (Ashanti)*

Whereas a liar takes one thousand years to go on a journey, the one who speaks the truth follows and overtakes the liar in a day.

*—Ghana (Akan)*

### ⧼⧽ TRUST

Befriend many but trust few. —*Uganda (Ganda)*

He who disappoints another is unworthy to be trusted.
—*Benin, Nigeria, Togo (Yoruba)*

Some people can be trusted for sure only after they
are buried. —*Ethiopia*

You can trust neither the sky in the rainy season
nor babies' bottoms! —*Africa*

Trusting in wealth is like looking for feathers on turtles.
—*Senegal*

The fattened sheep that trusts its owner lets its fatty tail
hang outside the barn door. —*Ethiopia*

He who puts his trust in people is like he who cups water
in his fingers. —*Ethiopia*

### ⧼⧽ RESPONSIBILITY

A child who is carried on the back won't know how far
the journey is. —*Nigeria (Njak)*

At whatever age a child gets a problem, at the same age
she has to shoulder the responsibility of solving it.
—*Nigeria (Igbo)*

An elephant's tusks are never too heavy for it to carry.
—*Zimbabwe*

The ant can carry the
corpses of other ants by
itself. —*Ethiopia*

It is the owner of the farm
who drives off a leopard,
not someone else.
—*Niger, Nigeria (Hausa)*

No matter how many
chores you finish in your
house, there is always yet
more to be done.
—*Mali (Bambara)*

Responsibility can also carry blame. —*South Africa*

The child who goes to the water hole to collect water
sometimes breaks the water pot. —*Ghana (Twi)*

One does not chop down the tree without picking up
some of its fruit. —*Ghana*

A thorn with which one has pricked oneself of one's
own accord does not pain. —*Kenya (Nyika)*

The one who suffers from overeating does not curse
his relatives. —*Kenya (Agikuyu)*

Those who blow on the fire will run from the smoke.
—*Burkina Faso (Mamprusi)*

Kindle not a fire that you cannot put out. —*Africa*

We do not look at another person's clock in order
to work. —*Benin, Nigeria, Togo (Yoruba)*

If you borrow a friend's hoe and work with it, wash it
and take it back to the owner.                    —*Ghana (Twi)*

Do not hold the mirror responsible for the image
it reflects.                                       —*Africa*

Do not drink ginger tea for other people's fever.
                                                   —*Tobago*

The one with a beak does not peck for another.
                                          —*Kenya (Agikuyu)*

When a box is carried, what's inside the box is
also carried.                                      —*Ghana*

If someone is unreliable, do not send him to do trading.
                                                   —*Ghana*

When the firstborn becomes foolish, the last born
inherits the cattle.                               —*Ethiopia*

Put you money where you mouth is.                  —*Jamaica*

A person has to die for what he has done.
                              —*Mozambique, Zimbabwe (Shona)*

When we came to help him bury his father, he gave us
the shovel and left.                               —*Africa*


## ⧪ WORK AND PRODUCTIVITY

A busy machete never rusts.                         —*Africa*

A chattering bird builds no nest.                  —*Burundi*

Talking about fire does not boil the pot.

—*United States (Black communities)*

Hand plow cannot make furrows by itself.

—*United States (Black communities)*

He who gets blisters from the hoe handle will not die
of hunger. —*Kenya, Tanzania, Rwanda*

A good tailor will sew even on New Year's Day.

—*East Africa (Kiswahili)*

A sleeping fox finds no meat. —*Brazil*

The dog that searches every stone will never be without
a bone. —*Namibia*

If you do not gather firewood, you cannot keep warm.

—*Angola, Namibia (Ovambo)*

The fire burns because of the wood gatherers. —*Mozambique*

If you do not scoop up the water, you do not scoop up
the fish. —*Ghana (Akan)*

Without overcoming bees, you cannot get honey.

—*East Africa (Kiswahili)*

No sweet without sweat. —*Uganda (Ganda)*

If you are healthy, ask for work. —*Tanzania (Zigula)*

He who takes wages for work needs to perform it.

—*West Africa (Fulani)*

If you want to eat in the evening, you have to work
during the day. —*Haiti*

Some stones are pretty when worn as necklaces, but who
is going to bore the hole in them? —*Nigeria (Igbo)*

A man who sits by the beach where fishermen make their
catch will never eat plain rice. —*Zambia*

If work were a good thing,
the rich would have grabbed
it a long time ago. —*Haiti*

The laborer is always in the
sun; the landowner is always
in the shade. —*Benin,*

*Nigeria, Togo (Yoruba)*

Whenever I work hard for
other people, I sleep on an
empty stomach.

—*Central Africa, East Africa, southern Africa*

*(Bantu)*

The stomach knows no day of rest.

—*Zimbabwe, Mozambique (Shona)*

So long as people are alive, there is no rest; they have
to work. —*Kenya (Agikuyu)*

Rest cannot shorten the way; going ahead does.

—*Mozambique (Tsonga)*

No bird flies and never rests. —*South Africa (Zulu)*

When the soap comes to an end, the washerwoman
rejoices.
*—Morocco*

If the hours are long enough and the pay is short
enough, someone will say it is women's work.
*—East Africa (Kiswahili)*

When mosquitoes work, they bite and then they sing.
*—Mali*

One who is serious all day will never have a good time,
while one who is frivolous all day will never establish
a household.
*—Egypt*

The seed that is sown is the one that sprouts.
*—Niger, Nigeria (Hausa)*

He who neglects his farm won't see a bright eye in
his house.
*—Niger, Nigeria (Hausa)*

The land is worth only so much as the person who
works it.
*—Haiti*

The earth is not thirsty for the blood of the warriors
but for the sweat of man's labor.
*—Brazil*

The hand suffers at work, but the mouth still must eat.
*—Sudan*

If you want to know how the hand is related to the
mouth, serve yourself a delicious meal.
*—Sudan*

To eat an egg, you must break the shell.
*—Jamaica*

The bird won't fly into your arrow.

*—Angola, Namibia (Ovambo)*

Ploughing superficially will only result in retracing
one's steps to pluck the weeds.                    —*Ethiopia*

Sending someone on an errand at mealtime is likely
to result in a botched message.                    —*Ethiopia*

Those who leave things undone until later are found with
them undone.                          —*Kenya (Agikuyu)*

An untouched drum does not speak.              —*Liberia (Jabo)*

Someone does not keep his hands between his thighs
and complain of poverty.                   —*Ghana (Akan)*

If you remain not at home, if you enter not, if you
appear not, you will find no work.          —*Senegal, Gambia (Wolof)*

The mule does not pull so well with a mortgage on
his back.                       —*United States (Black communities)*

The volunteer is worth ten pressed men.
                                  —*Niger, Nigeria (Hausa)*

It is better to work and be free than to be fed in captivity.
                                                  —*Gabon*

The able blacksmith will never lack work.       —*DRC (Mayombe)*

Only the young are patient under hard work.
                                  —*Niger, Nigeria (Hausa)*

When you get older, you keep warm with the wood you
gathered as a youth.                     —*Mali (Bambara)*

Lack of money is lack of friends; if you have money at
your disposal, every dog and goat will claim to be related
to you.
—Benin, Nigeria, Togo (Yoruba)

A wealthy man will always have followers.
—Nigeria

A man with wealth will always get a servant.
—Niger, Nigeria (Hausa)

No one in the presence of a large sum of money goes
hungry to bed.
—Ghana (Akan)

The rich eat without any fuss.
—Benin, Nigeria, Togo (Yoruba)

You shouldn't hoard your money and die of hunger.
—Ghana (Twi)

If one wants to eat, she asks her purse.
—Ghana (Twi)

If someone says he will give you something sweet to eat
and he gives you money, he has done it.
—Ghana (Twi)

Food can be refused after I have had my fill, but
not money.
—Mozambique, Zimbabwe (Shona)

If ten cents does not go out, it does not bring in
one thousand dollars.
—Ghana (Twi)

Make some money, but do not let money make you.
—Tanzania

Money can buy bed, not sleep; food, not appetite;

medicine, not health; book, not knowledge; house, not
home; woman, not wife; intimacy, not love; luxury,
not beauty.                                          *—Africa*

If you befriend rich people and you are in need,
your need will not be great.                    *—Ghana (Akan)*

One cannot count on riches.                        *—Somalia*

Money has wings.                              *—Ghana (Akan)*

Money does not stay in one place.             *—Ghana (Akan)*

Money no grow on tree.                            *—Jamaica*

Those who inherit fortunes are frequently more of
a problem than those who made them.              *—Congo*

If you are rich, always shut your door.          *—Ghana (Twi)*

Much wealth brings many enemies.        *—East Africa (Kiswahili)*

The one who overspent his resources troubled the
one who saved.                              *—Kenya (Agikuyu)*

Money that has no leisure is not given out as a loan.
                                               *—Ghana (Akan)*

Wealth is invited, but poverty invites itself.
                                 *—Zimbabwe, Mozambique (Shona)*

Lacking money is not [necessarily the same as]
being poor.                          *—Kenya, Tanzania, Rwanda*

Save money, and money will save you.             *—Jamaica*

Money is sharper than a sword.       *—Ghana (Ashanti)*

Money cannot talk, yet it can make lies look true.

*—South Africa*

Savings won't rot.       *—East Africa (Kiswahili)*

Money is not counted well for you by somebody else.

*—Uganda (Ganda)*

Money given to a mere lover is like money given to
a prostitute.       *—Africa*

If a child is entrusted with a large amount of money,
he will incur big debts.       *—Ghana (Twi)*

The elder who has no money is considered to be unwise.

*—Benin, Nigeria, Togo (Yoruba)*

You become wise when you begin to run out of money.

*—Ghana*

Wealth diminishes with use; learning increases with use.

*—Nigeria (Nupe)*

Wealth usually comes in walking but exits running.

*—Ethiopia*

Money is not the medicine against death.     *—Ghana (Akan)*

## ❀ POVERTY

The medicine of poverty is strength. —*Uganda (Ganda, Lugbara)*

Poverty destroys a man's reputation.

—*Benin, Nigeria, Togo (Yoruba)*

The poor man's word is considered last. —*South Africa (Zulu)*

The poor person's grievances are handled hastily.

—*Ghana (Akan)*

A poor man's drum is his belly. —*Niger, Nigeria (Hausa)*

If it were ever to rain soup, the poor would only
have forks. —*Brazil*

The poor eat meat when they bite their tongues.

—*Brazil*

The hen of a poor person does not lay eggs, and even if
she lays eggs, she never hatches, and if she hatches, she
never rears the chicks, and when
she rears, the chicks are taken by
the hawk. —*East Africa (Kiswahili)*

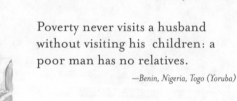

Poverty never visits a husband
without visiting his children: a
poor man has no relatives.

—*Benin, Nigeria, Togo (Yoruba)*

The poor man's children make the
rich man's children fat.

—*Uganda (Ganda)*

It is better to be poor in youth than in old age.

—Kenya (Kuria)

If you do not want to resign yourself to poverty, resign
yourself to work.

—Niger, Nigeria (Hausa)

Poverty is like a lion; if you do not fight, you get eaten.

—Tanzania (Haya)

Poverty teaches you the nature of people.

—Ghana (Akan)

The poor man has no time for illness.

—Mozambique

A poor person never goes bankrupt.

—Kenya (Agikuyu)

The one who is poor but owes nothing is not poor.

—Kenya (Agikuyu)

If a poor person has nothing else, he/she has at least
a sweet tongue with which to defer the payment of his/
her debts.

—Ghana (Akan, Twi)

The poor person does not experience poverty all
the time.

—Ghana (Akan)

Poor people entertain with the heart.

—Haiti

Poverty teaches courtesy.

—South Africa

The monkey says that there is nothing like poverty
for taking the conceit out of a man.

—Ghana (Ashanti)

## ✻ DEBT

Everyone is a debtor to someone, either in cash or
in kind.                                    —*Africa*

A promise is like a debt.                   —*Africa*

Never promise a poor person, and never owe a rich one.
                                            —*Brazil*

Debts do not decay; they get moldy.    —*Uganda (Ganda, Lugbara)*

One should not make one's suffering an excuse for
not paying a debt.                          —*Ghana (Akan)*

The rule for debts is to pay them.    —*East Africa (Kiswahili)*

If you pay what you owe, you get peace of mind.
                                            —*Ghana (Twi)*

The man who has paid tax is not afraid of the authorities.
                                            —*Mozambique*

The borrower who does not pay gets no more money
lent to him.                                —*Nigeria (Efik)*

A debtor does not get angry.                —*Ghana (Ga)*

Old debt better than old grudge.            —*Jamaica*

Borrowing is sweet; bitter is the day of payment.
                                            —*Niger, Nigeria (Hausa)*

The tongue with which the debtor puts off a debt is
different from that with which he asks for a loan.

*—Ghana*

While making a loan to somebody, you might be in
a sitting posture, but to request the loan back you will
have to get up. *—Uganda (Ganda)*

Lending is ruinous to lenders and borrowers. *—Egypt*

If someone does not go and buy something from
someone, then no one owes anyone a debt. *—Africa*

To want something and get it all leads to debt.

*—Ghana (Akan)*

Going to bed without dinner better than waking
up in debt. *—Jamaica*

If you take a loan to pay your debt, it is as if you were
to dig a hole to fill a hole. *—Ghana (Akan)*

A debtor who borrows to pay is still a debtor. *—Africa*

Because I owe you does not mean I cannot pound
grain in my own yard. *—Gambia (Mandinka)*

The unexpected payment of an old debt is a real
blessing for the creditor. *—Ghana*

## ❈ EVIL AND SHAME

Old Satan couldn't get along without plenty of help.

*—United States (Black communities)*

Evil is not good, but everyone indulges in it a bit.

*—Ghana (Akan)*

He who is bent on tasting evil will certainly get
a mouthful.  *—Kenya (Agikuyu)*

Without retaliation, evil would one day become extinct
from the world.  *—Nigeria*

Evil enters like a needle and spreads like an oak tree.

*—Ethiopia*

Evil follows the footsteps of the owner.  *—Uganda (Ganda, Lugbara)*

Doctor medicine cannot cure bad mind.  *—Guyana*

He who knows not shame does whatever he likes.

*—Egypt*

For one day a person may behave disgracefully; then for
all his life he is put to shame.  *—Benin, Nigeria, Togo (Yoruba)*

Shame don't break the neck of the person feeling
ashamed; it cause the person to bow he head.  *—Guyana*

Trouble don't set up like rain.

*—Antigua, Belize, Guyana, Jamaica, U.S. Virgin Islands*

Crime leaves a trail like a water beetle; like a snail,
it leaves its silver track; like a horse mango, it leaves
its smell.

—*Malawi*

Where there is sea, there will always be pirates. —*Malawi*

Eat with the devil, but give him a long spoon. —*Jamaica*

One who has revealed evil has caused the truth
to come out.

—*Mozambique, Zimbabwe (Shona)*

When the angels present themselves, the devils abscond.

—*Egypt*

## ✳ GREED AND THEFT

Greed will take you where you wouldn't be.

—*West Africa (Fulani)*

If you like too much good soup, you are always in debt.

—*Ghana (Akan)*

The abundance of fruit caused the death of fruit lover.

—*Tanzania*

Is big eye make the elephant swallow the calabash.

—*Caribbean*

A tree belonging to a greedy man bore abundantly,
but instead of gathering the fruit little by little, he took
an ax and cut it down that he might get all at once.

—*Benin, Nigeria, Togo (Yoruba)*

Too large a morsel chokes the child. —*Mauritania*

Do not take another mouthful before you have swallowed
what is in your mouth. —*Madagascar*

No one can hunt two birds at the same time.
—*Cameroon (Yaoundé)*

If you eat all your harvest, you won't have seed
for tomorrow. —*Africa*

Lust for gold has turned many a good man into
an animal. —*Haiti*

If greedy, wait. Hot will cool. —*Barbados*

If you steal food, eat in a dark corner. —*Zimbabwe*

A thief is a thief whether he steals an orange
or a diamond. —*Africa*

The hyena steals from sheer habit. —*Angola*

Light is the poison of thieves. —*Uganda (Ganda, Lugbara)*

A thief in your village is like a flea in your vest. —*DRC*

A thief is just as bad as a murderer. —*Kenya (Agikuyu)*

The thief who does not get caught passes off as
an honorable person. —*Haiti*

If you keep the company of thieves, you will become one.
—*Congo*

One thief never like to see another thief carry long bag.
—*Jamaica*

When thieves fight among themselves, the loot will be
found and returned.
*—Angola*

He who steals in the company of a woman will live
in fear until she dies.
*—Kenya (Agikuyu)*

If a thief says he knows how to steal, let him steal
a cannon.
*—Ghana (Ga)*

If you are teaching yourself to steal, teach yourself
to run.
*—Tanzania (Sukuma)*

## ✻ PRIDE AND VANITY

Crow does fly high, but when he come down, the ants
does still eat out he eye.
*—Barbados*

When a vulture is swept away by a strong wind, he claims
he is only playing.
*—Sierra Leone (Koranko)*

Cock, stop showing off. We all came out of the eggshell.
*—Ghana (Twi)*

We hear better cock than you crow.
*—Belize, Trinidad and Tobago*

The drum makes a great fuss because it is empty.
*—Trinidad and Tobago*

If you have never been to another man's farm, you say,
"I am the best farmer."
*—Ghana (Twi)*

Donkey got big ears, but he don't hear he own story.
*—Barbados, Guyana, Tobago*

Don't put yourself in a barrel when matchbox can
hold you.
—Antigua

He who wears too fine clothes shall go about in rags.
—Mauritania

Scornful dog eat dirty pudding.
—Barbados, Guyana

The frog wanted to be as big as the elephant, and burst.
—Ethiopia

The higher monkey climb is the more him expose
him behind.
—Caribbean

If you look beyond your eyebrows, you get lost.
—Ghana (Twi)

Pride goes only as far as one can spit.
—Congo

## ❋ HUMILITY

What you throw away standing up you will have to pick
up bending.
—Ethiopia

A back does not break from bending.
—Egypt

Bowing down to someone does not make you a
short man.
—Nigeria

To be humble when we need help is manliness.
—Egypt

If you are modest, you are modest to your own
advantage.
—Benin, Nigeria, Togo (Yoruba)

Even the mightiest eagle comes down to the treetops
to rest.
—Uganda (Ganda)

However you may run, you will have to stop.

*—Gambia (Mandinka)*

Even animals with four legs do sometimes fall. *—Africa*

There is no foot that does not stumble. *—South Africa (Zulu)*

Though a tree grows ever so high, the falling leaves
return to its roots.

*—Malawi*

If you climb up a tree, you must climb down the
same tree.

*—Sierra Leone*

A dog lowers its tail in the home of others.

*—Uganda (Ganda, Lugbara)*

Lower your head modestly while passing, and you
will harvest bananas.

*—Congo*

A cripple does not start a war song. *—Ghana (Ewe)*

Horse never too good to carry him own grass. *—Jamaica*

Slippery ground does not recognize kings.

*—Kenya, Uganda (Luhya)*

The most fragrant of flowers are eaten by the greenfly.

*—Malawi*

Do not praise your work in the field when they see it
with their own eyes.

*—Uganda (Ganda)*

The one who asks for a knife wants it to be known that
he has slaughtered a beast.

*—Mozambique, Zimbabwe (Shona)*

If you get rich, be in a dark corner when you jump
for joy. —*South Africa (Zulu)*

A tiger does not have to proclaim its tigritude. —*Nigeria*

Salt does not say of itself, "I am tasty." —*Ghana (Twi)*

Whatever accomplishment you boast of in the world,
there is someone better than you. —*Niger, Nigeria (Hausa)*

Cover up the good you do—do like the Nile and
conceal your sources. —*Egypt*

The humble pay for the mistakes of their betters. —*Mali*

Looking at the king's mouth, you will never think
he sucked his mother's breast. —*Nigeria*

The humblest calf suck the most milk. —*Jamaica*

Only scratch where you can reach. —*Kenya*

Be unable to handle an ax, but do not be unable
to handle instruction. —*Tanzania (Sukuma)*

If you go to a town and find its chief sitting on
the ground, you do not ask for a stool. —*Ghana (Akan)*

## ❋ INSIGHT AND INTROSPECTION

Losing one's eyesight is not as bad as losing one's insight.
—*Africa*

A man is what he thinks. —*Mali*

If one comes to a fork of the road in a strange country,
she stops to think.
*—Liberia (Jabo)*

All heads are the same, but not all thoughts are the same.
*—Ghana (Twi)*

Thoughts are quicker than gazelles.
*—Mali*

Examine long; be in the right long.
*—Madagascar (Malagasy)*

He who asks questions cannot avoid the answers.
*—Cameroon*

There is bound to be a knot in a very long string.
*—Ghana*

When one man's trouble has come, another man's
trouble is on the way.
*—Ghana (Twi)*

The enemy outside is no match for the enemy at home;
one is done in one's own home.
*—Benin, Nigeria, Togo (Yoruba)*

You can measure the depth of the sea, but what about
a man's heart?
*—Malawi*

Only the knife knows the heart of a pineapple.
*—Haiti*

Who hold the iron feel the heat.
*—Tobago*

We work on the surface. The depths are a mystery.
*—West Africa*

The best way to keep a secret is not to tell it to anyone.

*—East Africa (Kiswahili)*

It is not everything a man has seen that he speaks of.

*—Ghana (Akan)*

If you like making hints, then your secrets will
be revealed. *—Ghana (Akan)*

Every best friend got a next best friend. *—Barbados*

All food is fit to eat, but not all words are fit to speak.

*—Haiti*

Only when you have crossed the river can you say the
crocodile has a lump on his snout. *—Ghana*

Fishes die by their mouths. *—Belize, Guyana, Saint Kitts*

Fish that nibble every bait soon get catch. *—Belize*

When eye don't see, mouth don't talk.

*—Guyana, U.S. Virgin Islands*

When the mouth stumbles, it is worse than the foot.

*—Ghana (Twi)*

The tongue is the neck's enemy. *—Egypt*

Confiding a secret to an unworthy person is like carrying
grain in a bag with a big hole. *—Ethiopia*

The bush in which you hide has eyes.                    —*Kenya (Gusii)*

When the Nile knows a secret, the desert will soon
know it too.                                           —*Ethiopia*

What you do secretly others see secretly.              —*Ghana (Twi)*

No one shoots his gun while he is hiding from
the enemy.                                             —*Ghana (Akan)*

He who is looking for a place to sleep does not tell
you that he wets the bed.                              —*Ghana*

A hunter does not tell all the story of the chase.
                                                       —*Ghana (Akan)*

A donkey does not give birth in public.       —*Gambia (Mandinka)*

A person changing his clothing always hides
while changing.                                        —*Kenya*

You can hide and buy land, but you cannot hide
and work it.                                           —*Barbados*

If you cannot get the handle of the knife, do not touch
the blade.                                             —*U.S. Virgin Islands*

A knife does not know who its master is.               —*Ghana*

A woman hides the penis, but she won't hide the belly.
                                                       —*Burkina Faso (Mamprusi)*

Tears cannot be seen in the pouring rain.              —*Mali*

The sun cannot be hidden.                              —*Egypt*

What remains secretly in my heart lets me
sleep peacefully at home.

—*Haiti*

The fence conceals the secrets of the household.

—*Ghana*

## ⫸ CONSEQUENCE, CAUSE, AND EFFECT

When a lion eats a bad person and it is not killed,
tomorrow it will eat a good person.

—*Zambia (Lozi)*

If the hunter forgets his gun, the lion chases him.

—*Ghana (Akan)*

A man does not run among thorns for nothing;
either he is chasing a snake or a snake is chasing him.

—*Benin, Nigeria, Togo (Yoruba)*

A snake does not bite a man
without a cause.

—*Ghana (Ashanti)*

A crab does not swim in hot
water unless it wants to
turn red.        —*Africa*

Dead hog not afraid of
boiling water.        —*Jamaica*

When water throw away, you
cannot pick it up.        —*Jamaica*

You cannot cross a river without getting wet.

*—South Africa (Zulu)*

Where there are birds, there is water. *—Namibia*

Where you see dead meat, you will see John Crow.

*—Jamaica*

If you want to get rid of the flies, throw the bad
meat away. *—Zambia*

If you don't want leaf fall on you, don't stay under tree.

*—Jamaica*

If you make yourself grass, jackass will eat you.

*—Barbados, Guyana*

If you dig a hole, take care you don't fall in it. *—Jamaica*

He who digs a grave for his enemy may be digging
it for himself.

*—Lesotho*

The same knife stick goat stick sheep. *—Jamaica*

If you destroy a bridge, be sure you can swim.

*—East Africa (Kiswahili)*

If fish learned to keep him mouth shut, fisherman
wouldn't catch him. *—Jamaica*

If the cockroach refuses to stay in its hole, the chicken
refuses to stay hungry. *—Nigeria (Annang)*

It is no use overfeeding a pig just before slaughtering
it because you want to eat good pork meat. *—Zimbabwe*

A rotten fish pollutes the whole kitchen.                    —*Senegal*

Ashes fly back into the face of him who throws them.

—*Nigeria*

Spit in the sky, it go fall back in you eye.    —*Trinidad and Tobago*

He who sows thorns must walk on them barefoot.

—*Morocco*

He who runs about the fields is in danger of falling
into a pit.                              —*Benin, Nigeria, Togo (Yoruba)*

There is no cure that does not have its price.      —*Kenya*

She got pregnant and wanted meat, so a pregnant cow
was killed for her. When she gave birth, she wanted milk,
and there was nothing to give her.         —*Ethiopia, Kenya (Oromo)*

As long as there are lice in the seams of the garment,
there must be bloodstains on the fingernails.

—*Benin, Nigeria, Togo (Yoruba)*

Anyone who dices onions should not complain
about watering eyes.                             —*Africa*

The pot will smell of that which is put into it.

—*East Africa (Kiswahili)*

He who asks questions cannot avoid the answers.

—*Burundi*

If fowl scratch up too much dirt, him run the risk
of finding him grandma skeleton.                  —*Jamaica*

One who slings mud gets himself soiled as well.      —*Africa*

If an elephant steps on a trap that is set, it does
not spring back.
*—Ghana (Twi)*

He who digs too deep for a fish may come out with
a snake.
*—Ethiopia*

When little boy put on big man trousers, he must take
what he get.
*—Barbados, Guyana*

When a child does what she is not supposed to do,
she suffers what she is not supposed to suffer.
*—Ghana (Twi)*

Something that spoil in the morning cannot come
good in the evening.
*—Jamaica*

No one cuts down a tree and expects fruit to remain
on it.
*—Ghana (Akan)*

When a tree dies at its roots, its branches dry up also.
*—East Africa (Kiswahili)*

A piece of thread may succeed in exposing a horrible
deed.
*—Africa*

If you pull a string, it may have something on the end.
*—Ghana (Akan)*

No finger put into the mouth will come without saliva.
*—Zimbabwe, Mozambique (Shona)*

If you want to eat roast plantain, you must be ready
to burn you finger.
*—Jamaica*

If you watch your pot, your food will not burn.
*—Niger*

Who have raw meat must look fire.
*—Jamaica*

You lit the fire; now the smoke hurts your eyes.

—*DRC (Tetela)*

Smoke from roasting meat does not irritate the eyes.

—*Zimbabwe, Mozambique (Shona)*

You don't jump out of frying pan and into fire.

—*Jamaica*

If you play with fire, you bound to get burned.

—*Trinidad and Tobago*

You do not reap full consequences of a deed at once.

—*Burundi, Angola (Umbundu)*

## EQUALITY AND EQUITY

When the sun rises, it rises for everyone.

—*Namibia (Ovambo), Cuba*

The moon does not appear in one place alone.

—*Ghana (Akan)*

A canoe does not know who is king. When it turns over,
everyone gets wet.　　　　　—*Madagascar (Malagasy)*

No matter how powerful a man, he cannot make rain
fall on his farm alone.　　　—*Africa*

If the wind blows, it enters at every crevice.　　—*Egypt*

Smoke does not affect honeybees alone; it affects
honey gatherers as well.　　　—*Liberia (Bassa)*

Today for me, tomorrow for you.    —*Jamaica, Trinidad and Tobago*

What happens to the turkey can happen to the
rooster, too.
                                   —*Haiti*

Famine strikes the adult as much as the child.
                                   —*Niger, Nigeria (Hausa)*

The green leaf falls; the withered one also falls.
                                   —*Ghana (Akan)*

Young tears will fall as freely as old tears fell.    —*Africa*

If it is dark, all men are black.    —*Ghana (Ga)*

If a tall man bends, he and a short person are alike.
                                   —*Ghana (Akan)*

Fishes swim toward those of the same size.
                                   —*Benin, Nigeria, Togo (Yoruba)*

A leopard licks its spots, black and white.    —*South Africa (Zulu)*

The stick that hit a black dog can hit a white one too.
                                   —*Guyana*

Dress according to your size, and associate with
your equal.
                                   —*Morocco*

The mule grazing with the horses imagines being
their equal.
                                   —*Somali*

People are equal only when they are walking.
                                   —*Kenya (Agikuyu)*

To obtain equality is not a month's job.    —*Kenya (Agikuyu)*

# ⚶ JUSTICE

Justice is like fire; even if you cover it with a veil, it still burns. 
*—Madagascar*

All of the justice in the world isn't fastened up in the courthouse. 
*—United States (Black communities)*

A good case is not difficult to state. 
*—Ghana (Ashanti)*

Judgment must wait to hear all the witnesses. 
*—Nigeria (Igbo)*

If you are unable to settle your case at home, then it is heard of outside. 
*—Ghana (Akan)*

You do not expect to win a case in someone else's village. 
*—Zambia (Kaonde)*

If chickens were judges, cockroaches would be sentenced. 
*—Jamaica*

Seeking redress in court is like putting your hand in a hornet's nest. 
*—Malawi*

In the land of no law, there is no offense. 
*—Africa*

If the fire of the law dies here and burns there, it is not operating properly. 
*—Ghana (Twi), Burundi*

If with the right hand you flog a child, with your left hand draw her unto your breast. 
*—Benin, Nigeria, Togo (Yoruba)*

Justice becomes injustice when it makes two wounds on a head that only deserves one.

—*Congo, Angola (Bakongo), DRC (Kongo)*

It is always a double punishment to beat a child and ask her not to cry.

—*Nigeria (Igbo)*

It is better to be the victim of injustice than to be unjust yourself.

—*Burundi*

People may pass judgment without knowing the truth; God always renders punishment, because he knows the whole truth.

—*Ethiopia*

Only death is just.

—*South Africa*

## ❋ PEACE, RESOLUTION, AND RECONCILIATION

It is better to build bridges than walls.

—*East Africa (Kiswahili)*

She/he learns reconciliation before knowing how to fight.

—*Ethiopia, Kenya (Oromo)*

To engage in conflict, one does not bring a knife that cuts but a needle that sews.

—*East Africa (Kiswahili)*

Allowing a current matter to remind one of similar matters in the past prevents a quarrel from ending easily.

—*Benin, Nigeria, Togo (Yoruba)*

Do not ever slam the door; you might want to go back.

—*Africa*

Taking aim for too long can ruin your eyes.

*—Niger, Nigeria (Hausa)*

The peacemaker receives the blows. *—Benin, Nigeria, Togo (Yoruba)*

A word of peace redeems a crime. *—Namibia (Ovambo)*

The road to peace is not far. *—Gambia (Mandinka)*

Every animal eats where it finds peace. *—Ghana*

Peace is more fattening than food. *—Namibia (Ovambo)*

A day of peace in times of stress is like a thousand days
in paradise. *—Nigeria*

Peace wins over wealth. *—Algeria*

Peace is costly but is worth the expense. *—Kenya (Agikuyu)*

Peace is the father of friendship. *—Benin, Nigeria, Togo (Yoruba)*

There is no peace until after enmity. *—Egypt*

There must be peace in the district to have law and order
in the country. *—Niger, Nigeria (Hausa)*

Peace and injustice are like night and day; they cannot
stay together. *—Nigeria*

If a person loves peace, it does not make her or him
a coward. *—Nigeria (Igbo)*

The value of peace is never known until the peace
is disturbed. *—Sierra Leone*

## ⪢ LOYALTY

Leopard does not eat leopard.
*—Ghana (Akan)*

The thief does not gossip about his accomplice.
*—Liberia (Jabo)*

He eats on both sides of the river like a water snake.
*—South Africa (Zulu)*

A bull is not known in two herds.
*—Zimbabwe*

We do not sleep at one side and fight for the other side.
*—Ghana (Akan)*

If crocodiles ate their own eggs, what would they do
to the flesh of a frog?
*—Nigeria*

If dog have too much master, him starve.
*—Belize, Guyana, Jamaica*

Your husband's faithfulness is tested when you are away.
*—Uganda (Ganda)*

## ⪢ COMMUNITY

One man's road does not go far without meeting
another's.
*—Ghana (Ashanti)*

A person is a person because of other persons.
*—Lesotho*

If two trees stand apart, they won't rub each other.
*—Ghana (Twi)*

The army of the palm tree is its branches.     —*Ghana*

A public gathering makes it impossible for a bully
to dominate.     —*Ghana (Akan)*

Although the black ants bite, they do not bite one
another.     —*Tanzania (Kuria)*

Never fight a stranger in the dark; he may turn out to
be your brother.     —*Zambia*

The town that never permits foreigners to mix with them
never becomes a big town.     —*Ghana*

Eat alone, hungry alone.     —*U.S. Virgin Islands*

Exile is the brother of death.     —*North Africa (Berber)*

One person does not build a town.     —*Ghana (Akan)*

One man cannot collect the crops.     —*Angola*

One tree does not make a forest.     —*Ghana (Twi)*

The slowest camel in the caravan sets the pace.     —*Somalia*

They who live as neighbors must be compassionate.
—*Kenya (Agikuyu)*

Choose your neighbors before you buy your house.
—*Nigeria*

If your neighbor's house burns, draw water for putting
out the fire on yours.     —*East Africa (Kiswahili)*

Sometimes, better your good neighbor who is close by than your relative who is far away.
—*Ethiopia*

If you sell a drum in your own village, you get the money and keep the sound.
—*Madagascar (Malagasy)*

It is one man who kills the elephant, but the whole town eats.
—*Ghana*

If one person kindles the fire, others can take live coals from it.
—*Ghana (Twi)*

However full the house, the hen finds a corner to lie in.
—*Sierra Leone*

"The heavens will fall" is not the concern of only one individual.
—*Benin, Nigeria, Togo (Yoruba)*

As long as you stay in a group, the lion will stay hungry.
—*Nigeria*

## ⊰⊱ UNITY AND COOPERATION

The multitude is stronger than the king.
—*Tunisia*

An elephant dies because of many spears.
—*Zambia (Luvale)*

Ants surrounded the dying elephant.
—*DRC*

Ants are tiny, but they lift things that are many times their size and weight.
—*Africa*

Fifty lemons may be a big load for one person but light decoration for fifty people.
—*Ethiopia*

If two people carry a log, it does not press hard on their
heads.                                          —Ghana (Twi)

If everyone helps to hold up the sky, then one person
does not become tired.                          —Ghana (Twi)

Numbers can achieve anything.                   —Ghana (Twi)

What is looked for by many will have a finder.
                                               —Uganda (Ganda)

When spiderwebs unite, they can tie up a lion.    —Ethiopia

The strength of ants is in their number.            —Africa

If you step on one ant, the others come to bite you, too.
                                                —West Africa

Ants build their anthills by riding on the backs of
one another.                                     —Ethiopia

Ants usually unite in greater numbers before they
can make noise.                                      —Africa

Rings sound when there are two.        —Zimbabwe (Ndebele)

The foot of the single person does not sound.
                                        —Uganda (Ganda, Lugbara)

One person alone does not arrest a lunatic.    —Ghana (Akan)

If one tree faces the storm alone, it collapses.   —Ghana (Twi)

Those who aren't united are beaten by a small boy.
                                               —Kenya (Agikuyu)

If the fingers of one hand quarrel, they cannot pick
up the food.
*—East Africa*

Teeth will never quarrel with the tongue. *—Niger, Nigeria (Hausa)*

A boat can never advance forward if each rower is
rowing his own way.
*—East Africa (Kiswahili)*

Sticks in a bundle are unbreakable. *—Tanzania, Kenya (Bondei)*

Unity among the cattle makes the lion lie down hungry.
*—Africa*

If all snakes lived together in one place, who would
approach them?
*—Africa*

The snakes' habit of not traveling in groups makes it
easy for humans to kill them with machetes.
*—Benin, Nigeria, Togo (Yoruba)*

If birds travel without
coordination, they beat
each other's wings
*—East Africa (Kiswahili)*

If I am helping you to make
your fence, why are you
hiding the string?
*—Ghana (Twi)*

That which is consumed
alone may be indigestible,
but that which is shared with
others is pleasantly
palatable. *—Ethiopia*

Where there is no jealousy, a small hare's leather is
enough to cover four people. —*Burundi (Rundi)*

You do not send someone to the top of a tree or a
high place and remove the ladder under him. —*Ghana (Twi)*

Where there is no common interest, there is no
general will. —*Africa*

Partnership in the trap, share of the meat. —*DRC (Mongo)*

When minds are the same, that which is far off will come.
—*East Africa*

Make a bed for the children of other people in the place
where your own children sleep. —*Morocco*

If you see an old woman is trouble, then there's nobody
taking care of her. —*Mali (Minyanka)*

A united family eats from the same plate. —*South Africa (Zulu)*

Unity is enduring, even if it is hard to come by. —*Ethiopia*

I am because we are. —*East Africa*

## ⋇ HELP AND ASSISTANCE

When you see a turtle on top of a fence post, you know
it had some help. —*Africa*

That which did not shout for help but waited patiently
died in the trap. —*Kenya, Uganda (Luhya)*

He who is pierced with thorns must limp off to him who
has a lancet. —*Benin, Nigeria, Togo (Yoruba)*

If two cheeks chew something, the job is quickly done.
—*Ghana (Akan)*

If you have no teeth, you will have to persuade others
to bite for you. —*Botswana, South Africa (Tswana)*

It is not the shooter alone who kills an animal.
—*Ghana (Akan)*

No one ties a knot without the thumb. —*Ghana*

Fire cannot cross a river without an ally.
—*Benin, Nigeria, Togo (Yoruba)*

If an ant is going to cross a stream, it is because of a stick.
—*Ghana (Akan)*

Cross the river in a crowd and the crocodile won't
eat you. —*Africa*

The insect that bites has no one to come to its aid
when it is in trouble. —*Africa*

Two small antelopes can beat one big one. —*Ghana (Twi)*

Two strong men will move a heavy stone. —*North Africa*

When the load fatigues the head, the shoulder takes over.
—*Nigeria (Igbo)*

Reinforcement beats the foe. —*Ghana (Twi)*

The person that we know in the daytime, we do not light
a lamp to see his face in the night.     *—Ghana (Akan)*

A tree is known by its fruit.     *—Nigeria*

A man's character cannot be washed off by the rain.

*—Africa*

Vast differences among people are in the realm
of character, not anatomy.     *—Ethiopia (Oromo)*

One's character is just like any writing on a stone—it
is obvious.     *—Liberia (Jabo)*

When the character of a man is not clear to you,
look at his friends.     *—Haiti*

Character is a line on stone; none can rub it out.

*—Niger, Nigeria (Hausa)*

Character is like pregnancy; you cannot hide it for long.

*—Africa*

No matter how good you treat hog and clean he skin,
loose he and he gone back to mud.     *—Grenada, Guyana*

If you talk with hog, you cannot expect anything
but grunt.     *—Jamaica*

God knew how the snake is and made it without legs.

*—Ethiopia, Kenya*

Cat catch rat, but he steal master fish too.     *—Barbados*

Every man honest till the day him get catch.　　　*—Jamaica*

No better herring, no better barrel.　　　*—Jamaica*

Small garden, bitter weed.　　　*—Barbados, Guyana*

Better you lose time than character.　　　*—Africa*

One loses one's reputation in one day, but the disgrace is
for all days.　　　*—Benin, Nigeria, Togo (Yoruba)*

If the spirit world possesses nothing else, it has at least
the power of its name.　　　*—Ghana (Ashanti)*

If there is character, ugliness becomes beauty; if there
is none, beauty becomes ugliness.　　　*—Nigeria*

Where you sit when you are old shows where you stood
in youth.　　　*—Benin, Nigeria, Togo (Yoruba)*

He who is free of faults will never die.　　　*—Congo*


## ❋ PATIENCE, PERSEVERANCE, AND PERSISTENCE

At the gate of patience there is no crowding.　　　*—Morocco*

Always being in a hurry does not prevent death; neither
does going slowly prevent living.　　　*—Nigeria (Igbo)*

Because you are in a hurry does not mean you were born
before your father and mother.　　　*—Ethiopia, Kenya (Oromo)*

Even a slow walker will arrive.　　　*—Senegal, Gambia (Wolof)*

A garden is like a babe; it does not grow fast.

—Zambia (Bemba)

Grain by grain, the hen's stomach is full. —Brazil

One-one coco full basket. —Jamaica

A patient person gains at last. —Nigeria (Igbo)

At the bottom of patience there is heaven.

—Chad, Niger, Nigeria (Kanuri)

Do not be impatient when you question, so that you
get angry when it is time to listen. —Egypt

If the person is already coming to you, do not say,
"Come on." —Ghana (Twi)

If you act in a hurried way, confusion will seek for you.

—Ghana (Akan)

If you become impatient with the housefly on your sore,
you injure yourself. —Ghana (Twi)

If you skin the ant with patience, you will see its
intestines. —Ghana (Twi)

Do not be in a hurry to swallow when chewing
is pleasant. —Malawi (Nyanja)

If there is a morsel of food in your mouth, you can wait
till what is on the fire is roasted. —Ghana (Twi)

He who restrains his impatience to eat will find his food
the sweeter. —Niger, Nigeria

Haste is the sister of repentance. —*Morocco*

Haste has no blessing. —*East Africa (Kiswahili)*

You cannot harvest vegetables quicker than they grow.
—*Ethiopia*

The impatient man eats raw food. —*Tanzania*

The patient man eats ripe fruits. —*East Africa (Kiswahili)*

You must eat an elephant one bite at a time. —*Ghana (Twi)*

While there is a mountain in your path, do not sit down
at its foot and cry. Get up and climb it. —*Africa*

Long road draw sweat; shortcut draw blood.
—*Grenada, Guyana, Jamaica, Saint Vincent*

We will water the thorn for the sake of the rose.
—*West Africa (Mandinka)*

A tree that hasn't been straightened up in thirty years
won't be straightened in a day. —*Ghana (Twi)*

Whoever plows with a team of donkeys must
have patience. —*Zimbabwe*

Only a man with patience will taste the milk of a
barren cow. —*Africa*

Taking time ain't laziness. —*Barbados*

Patience removes mountains. —*Ghana (Akan)*

Patience leads to solving a problem. —*Ghana (Akan)*

To see a snail's eyes, one must be very patient.
*—Africa*

To the patient man will come all the riches of the world.
*—Liberia*

Do not hurry the night; the sun will always rise for its own sake.
*—Eritrea*

The moon moves slowly, but it crosses the town.
*—Ghana (Ashanti)*

If you wait for tomorrow, tomorrow comes. If you do not wait for tomorrow, tomorrow comes.
*—Liberia (Malinke)*

## ❋ RESPECT AND RECIPROCITY

Every rope got two ends.
*—Barbados*

The key that opens is also the key that locks.
*—Angola, Congo, DRC (Kongo)*

The old woman cares for the hen, and the hen cares for the old woman.
*—Ghana (Twi)*

Do not laugh at a distant boat being tossed by the waves. Your relatives may be in it.
*—Kenya (Luhya)*

Don't sit on the riverbed and talk the river bad.
*—Trinidad and Tobago*

The dog that you did not feed will not hear your call.
*—DRC*

If your cow gives you milk, do not let it suffer thirst.

*—Africa*

If you ride the horse, you must pay to shoe him.

*—Jamaica*

Till you are across the river, beware how you insult the mother alligator.

*—Haiti*

One camel does not make fun of the other camel's hump.

*—Guinea*

The teeth of the one who laughs too much will turn brown.

*—Uganda (Ganda, Lugbara)*

One should never laugh at a sick person; perhaps what afflicts him today may afflict you tomorrow.

*—Benin, Nigeria, Togo (Yoruba)*

One does not give the advice "stand up straight" to a humpback.

*—Benin, Nigeria, Togo (Yoruba)*

You do not cut to pieces your ally's shield and then say to him, "Help me."

*—Ghana (Twi)*

If a person shaves you with a razor, do not shave him with broken glass.

*—Suriname*

Do not be like the mosquito that bites the owner of the house.

*—Malawi*

When the bee comes to your house, let her have beer; you may want to visit the bee's house someday.

*—DRC*

If you are always in the habit of being other people's guest, you must be the host one day.

*—Africa*

If someone sweats for you, you change his shirt.    —*Haiti*

If your parents took care of you when you were teething,
you should take care of them when they are losing
their teeth.    —*Africa*

The hide that served the mother to carry the child will
serve the child to carry the mother.    —*Congo (Mboshi)*

The brother or sister who does not respect the traditions
of the elders won't be allowed to eat with the elders.
    —*Ghana (Ga)*

If the elders leave you a legacy of dignified language, you
do not abandon it and speak childish language.    —*Ghana (Twi)*

He who upsets something should know how to put it
back again.    —*Sierra Leone*

Never pick up what you did not put down.
    —*U.S. Virgin Islands*

Never kick down the ladder you climb on.
    —*Trinidad and Tobago*

The creator of a dance should not be excluded from it.
    —*Ghana (Akan)*

Dance with the one who brought you.
    —*United States (Black communities)*

If he who says "Let us go" says "Let us return," you do
not refuse him.    —*Ghana (Akan)*

If someone says he will carry you, you do not say,
"I will walk."    —*Ghana (Akan)*

If the mouth slips, the consequence is worse than when
the foot slips.
—*Ghana (Twi)*

To call in a bad mood brings about a moody reply.
—*Ethiopia, Kenya (Oromo)*

Two jackass don't bray at the same time.
—*Antigua, Jamaica*

He who shares your food but does not share your tasks
is a freeloader; he who eats the sweet should also eat
the sour.
—*Benin, Nigeria, Togo (Yoruba)*

Don't let nobody take bread out of you mouth when they
can't even give you biscuit.
—*Barbados, Guyana, Montserrat*

A wound given in public is stitched in public.
—*Kenya (Agikuyu)*

Familiarity breeds contempt; distance secures respect.
—*Benin, Nigeria, Togo (Yoruba)*

A river makes the most noise when it knows that the sea
is far away.
—*Africa*

If you are taller than your father, that does not make you
his peer.
—*Malawi*

Before you ask a man for clothes, look at the clothes that
he is wearing.
—*Nigeria (Yoruba)*

When the hunter comes from the bush carrying
mushrooms, he is not asked for news of his hunting.
—*Ghana (Ashanti)*

The fruit tree is treated with respect.
—*South Africa (Zulu)*

Mock the palm tree only when the date harvest is over.

—*Ethiopia*

The digger of the well is not forbidden the water.

—*East Africa (Kiswahili)*

A storm may destroy the fields, but bad manners
will destroy the nation.

—*Africa*

Learn politeness from the impolite.

—*Egypt*

A good mouth blesses itself.

—*Ghana (Twi)*

Respect is mutual.

—*South Africa (Zulu)*

Respect depends on reciprocity.

—*Cameroon (Nyang)*

## ⊷ GENEROSITY, GIVING, AND RECEIVING

Generosity is wealth.

—*Africa*

What you give to others bears fruit for you.

—*Senegal*

Richness of spirit and heart begets richness of cloth and
coin.

—*Cameroon*

People who share with others are seldom hungry.

—*Haiti*

Children of generous people do not die of hunger.

—*Africa*

He who will not give you a bone will not give you meat.

—*Namibia (Ovambo)*

The calculating spirit destroys real generosity.

—Kenya (Agikuyu)

The hand that gives is better than the one that receives.

—Algeria

A pint of help better than a thousand pities.

—Guyana, U.S. Virgin Islands

A candle burns itself out to give light to others.     —Africa

If you have, give; if you need, seek.     —Malawi

Better the smallest present than the most magnificent
meanness.

—Niger, Nigeria (Hausa)

Give your words with your goods and it will make
two gifts.

—Egypt

Giving badly is the same as absolutely refusing.

—DRC, Zambia (Lamba)

A genteel refusal is preferable to an uncivil gift.     —Haiti

Giving is a matter of the heart; do not say it is a matter
of wealth.

—East Africa (Kiswahili)

However little a person gives, he is on your side.

—Uganda (Ganda)

He who gives to you stores; he who refuses you buries.

—Uganda (Ganda)

Giving to her who has given you something is not giving
but paying. Giving to her who does not give you
something is not giving; it is throwing away.

—East Africa (Kiswahili)

Giving to oneself is better than receiving.

—*Angola, Namibia (Ovambo)*

A giver and a receiver—who is more burdened?

—*East Africa (Kiswahili)*

Accept if you give.

—*East Africa (Kiswahili)*

## ⁂ KINDNESS AND GOOD DEEDS

There is no beauty but the beauty of action.

—*Morocco*

A kind person is the one who is kind to strangers.

—*DRC (Bakongo)*

A good deed will make a good neighbor.

—*Central Africa, East Africa, southern Africa (Bantu)*

Kindness allows a person to eat food he did not buy.

—*Ghana (Akan)*

Greet everyone cordially when you do not know who
your in-laws are going to be.

—*Madagascar*

All the deeds a man has done will come back to haunt
his son.

—*Africa*

Kindness can pluck the hairs of a lion's mustache.

—*Sudan*

Kindness is the best remedy for suffering.

—*Mozambique*

Goodwill makes the road shorter.

—*Brazil*

It is better to walk than to grow angry with the road.

*—Senegal, Gambia (Wolof)*

To go where there is no road is better than to remain without doing anything.

*—Senegal, Gambia (Wolof)*

A person is like the long grass: if you treat it well, it grows well; if you do not, it spoils.

*—Ghana (Akan)*

At times, one day's mistake can loom larger than a year of good deeds.

*—Ethiopia*

If someone's eyes are red, do not slap him in the face.

*—Ghana (Twi)*

He who has done you a kindness should never be ill used.

*—Benin, Nigeria, Togo (Yoruba)*

A good deed is something one returns.

*—Guinea*

Good deeds never spoil.

*—East Africa (Kiswahili)*

## GOODNESS

Nothing is so good that it cannot be improved.

*—Kenya (Agikuyu)*

If something is not good, then we make it good.

*—Ghana (Akan)*

Nobody can see his own goodness; it can be seen only by others.

*—Kenya (Agikuyu)*

In a place where good is done, bad deeds are seen at once.

*—East Africa (Kiswahili)*

A white cloth and a stain never agree.

—Benin, Nigeria, Togo (Yoruba)

Goodness is done by a bad person; evil cannot be
done by a good person.          —East Africa (Kiswahili)

Ordinary people are as common as grass, but good
people are dearer than an eye.     —Benin, Nigeria, Togo (Yoruba)

The sin for which you repent is the father of virtue; but a
virtue that you talk about is the mother of sin.     —Africa

Nothing is completely bad.          —Lesotho

Evil does not last, but good does.     —Kenya (Agikuyu)


### ⁂ GRATITUDE

God does not allow anyone to suffer without leaving
a gap for thankfulness.          —Nigeria (Igbomina)

Do not blame God for having created the tiger, but
thank Him for not having given it wings.

—Ethiopia (Amharic)

Who gives not thanks to men gives not thanks to God.

—Egypt

Gratitude is what shows whether a gift is appreciated.

—Niger, Nigeria (Hausa)

Remember the rain that made your corn grow.     —Haiti

Be grateful to the tree so that it may yield more fruits.

—Mozambique, Zimbabwe (Shona)

A well-educated man always has a kind word to say about the place where he spends the night.         —North Aftica (Berber)

Never eat and forget.         —Barbados

The piece of meat cannot be so sweet that you forget the cook who roasted it.         —Kenya, Uganda (Luhya)

The dog is foolish but wise to remember the person who gave it food.         —Africa

One who teaches you how to set a trap, won't you give her of the meat you catch?         —Uganda (Ganda)

If you borrow an ax, return it with some of the ribs it has cut.         —South Africa (Zulu)

You cannot use a wild banana leaf to shield yourself from the rains and then tear it to pieces later when the rains come to an end.         —Kenya (Nandi)

A forest that has sheltered you, you should not call a patch of scrub.         —Ghana (Twi)

Thanks are due to the shoulders that keep the shirt from slipping off.         —Benin, Nigeria, Togo (Yoruba)

The one-eyed man thanks God only when he sees a man blind in both eyes.         —Nigeria

The man with a miserable life is never tired of it.         —Ghana (Ewe)

To express thanks is to provide for one's future.         —South Africa (Zulu)

Do not dirty the place where you have eaten. —*Malawi*

Do not despise a gift, no matter how small it is. —*Lesotho*

Never curse bridge that you cross. —*Barbados*

Kick away the ladder and your feet are left dangling.
—*Malawi*

When man belly full, he break up the pot. —*Guyana*

When people eat eggs, they do not remember the pains
the hen underwent while laying them. —*Africa*

An ungrateful person eats fast and wipes his lips.
—*Ghana (Akan)*

You have cured his testicles, and he has used them on
your wife. —*Uganda (Ganda)*

Having recovered from his illness, he forgot his God.
—*Ethiopia*

The one who has helped others climb the ladder
gets kicked in the teeth. —*East Africa (Kiswahili)*

He who installs a king never rules with him.
—*South Africa (Zulu)*

A donkey always says "thank you" with a kick. —*Kenya*

If you receive a gift, do not measure it. —*Kenya*

Cow never know the use of him tail till him lose it.
—*Jamaica*

The one being carried does not realize how far away
the town is.

—Nigeria

Man counts what he is refused, not what he is given.

—Kenya (Agikuyu)

The man who eats with a spoon does not remember
that he once ate with his fingers.

—Congo

Get motorcar do not mean throw away bicycle.

—Guyana

Man no finish climb hill should never throw away
the stick.

—Jamaica

Give thanks for a little and you'll find a lot.

—Niger, Nigeria (Hausa)

No throw away dirty water till you get clean.

—Bahamas, Guyana, U.S. Virgin Islands

A toad will realize the importance of water only when the
pond gets dry.

—Zambia

Do not tell the man who is carrying you that he stinks.

—Sierra Leone

How can you like the firewood and dislike the gatherer?

—Uganda (Ganda)

We ain't what we want to be; we ain't what we gonna be;
but thank God, we ain't what we was.

—United States (Black communities)

# ✳ COURAGE AND BRAVERY

What is left by the trembling one is taken by the one who climbs the tree.

—Angola, Namibia (Ovambo)

When a needle falls into a deep well, many people will look into the well, but few will be ready to go down after it.

—Guinea

Is heart, not horn, that make ram goat brave.

—Guyana

The courageous one sheds blood; the coward sweats.

—Uganda (Ganda, Lugbara)

The coward died from the heat of the cooking pot.

—Uganda (Ganda, Lugbara)

Even over cold pudding, the coward says, "It will burn my mouth."

—Ethiopia

Bravery in the house is no bravery.

—Ghana (Akan)

Who is brave enough to tell the lion that his breath smells?

—North Africa (Berber)

It is easy to cut to pieces a dead elephant, but no one dares attack a live one.

—Benin, Nigeria, Togo (Yoruba)

When a man's coat is threadbare, it is easy to pick a hole in it.

—Ghana

Courage isn't the same as fighting someone stronger than you.

—East Africa (Kiswahili)

If you chase away a coward and you do not give him room to flee, he shows you his strength.                    —*Ghana (Twi)*

Strength does not correspond with courage.

—*Kenya (Agikuyu)*

The little ant at its hole is full of courage.    —*Zambia (Bemba)*

One man you can trust is better than an army
of cowards.                                                          —*Egypt*


### ❈ AUTHENTICITY

Follow the saint no farther than his doorstep.          —*Egypt*

Not all who go to church house go there to pray.

—*Barbados*

A cat goes to a monastery, but she still remains a cat.

—*Congo*

Not every dreadlocks is a Rasta, and not every Rasta is
a dreadlocks.                                              —*Jamaica*

The twig that falls in the water will never become a fish.

—*Niger, Nigeria (Hausa)*

No matter how long a log floats on the river, it will never
be a crocodile.                                    —*Mali (Bambara)*

A donkey cannot get rid of its large ears merely by
shaking its head vigorously.                            —*Gambia*

A sheep cannot bleat in two different places at the same time.

*—Tanzania*

One does not claim kinship with a person and yet split the person's thighs.

*—Benin, Nigeria, Togo (Yoruba)*

Soap and water clean you hand but not you heart.

*—Guyana, U.S. Virgin Islands*

If you pledge your tongue, you cannot get it back.

*—Ghana (Twi)*

Nobody can use another person's teeth to smile.

*—Kenya (Kalenjin)*

He cries with one eye.

*—South Africa (Zulu)*

Is it not with saying "honey" that sweetness will come into the mouth.

*—Africa*

A priest sees people at their best, a lawyer at their worst, but a doctor sees them as they really are.

*—Congo*

## JOY AND HAPPINESS

To be happy in one's home is better than to be a chief.

*—Africa*

A smiling face removes unhappiness.

*—Niger, Nigeria (Hausa)*

The place where you are happy is better than the place where you were born.

*—Ghana (Twi)*

Happiness requires something to do, something to love, and something to hope for. —*East Africa (Kiswahili)*

Happiness is dancing when the drumming is good. —*South Africa*

Happiness is the greatest doctor in the world. —*Haiti*

The fault of happiness is its finishing. —*Niger, Nigeria (Hausa)*

Elderhood

In Africa, older persons are valued for their age and experience. So when my friend Yao went to study in Britain, he was amazed to find a society that was preoccupied with youthful beauty and fearful of old age. As far as Yao was then aware, "You can run quicker than an old man, but for his wisdom and his words, you are behind" (Tanzania).

He was more than appalled when he discovered that British families would put away aging parents in old people's homes and seem to forget them there. However, by the time Yao returned to his home country, Ghana, he was questioning whether "the tongue of experience holds the most truth" (Egypt). Ghanaians called someone like Yao a "been-to," a term describing foreign-educated elites who feel they have to choose one culture over the other.

Yao became a judge in Ghana, with the status and lifestyle that were once reserved for colonial rulers only. However, Yao fell short when his village assessed him. His SUV, chauffeur, designer clothes, Oxbridge accent, and social calendar might have impressed his fellow been-tos. However, on his visits to his village, he had to accept a place below elders who had no formal schooling and few material possessions.

Ghanaian councils of elders carried such weight

that these bodies remained intact under colonial rule. These councils so valued their role that they gave rise to the Ethiopian proverb "Better to keep an elderly person from dinner than from council."

Yao's knowledge was not in doubt. He had facts, experience, and skills needed to administer British law. However, Yao's community believed that he still lacked wisdom—he needed time to add discretion and intuitive understanding to his knowledge. Yao therefore had no voice in village affairs. "Where there is an old man, one does not ask the advice of a young man" (Togo).

Yao and the council of elders judged cases differently. For example, if Yao ruled on a case of assault, he might release the innocent or punish the guilty with a fine or a prison term. The elders would go beyond punishing or releasing the offender, seeking to undo harm to all concerned. They might advise or compensate the living and follow a ritual (such as sacrificing a sheep) to appease the departed. In addition, while Yao was usually the sole judge in his court, the elders ruled collectively, because "knowledge is like the ocean; no man's arms can embrace it" (Kiswahili).

Elders sat in council beyond their obviously productive phase because, as the Namibians say, "though a tree does not bear fruit, it is not cut down." They continued to garner respect no matter their physical appearance because "the mouth of the elderly man is without teeth, but never without words of wisdom" (Kiswahili).

Like many other been-tos, Yao led one life on his

job in the city and another on his visits to his village. He accepted that as far as his elders were concerned, he would have to wait until age gave him standing in his village. As a Jamaican proverb says, "young yam can't make soup."

# ❊ AGE, ELDERS, AND EXPERIENCE

Old age does not announce itself. —South Africa (Zulu)

Old age eats youth. —Kenya (Agikuyu)

Old age has one mouth. —Uganda (Ganda, Lugbara)

Everyone has been a child before, but not everyone has been an old person. —Ghana (Akan)

A mother lying down sees farther than a child in a tree. —Sierra Leone (Krio)

When a child is cutting a tree, it is the elderly person who knows where the tree will fall. —Africa

Every time an old man dies, it is as if a library has burned down. —West Africa

Better to keep an elderly person from dinner than from council. —Ethiopia

If we are going to purify the people, an elder is never absent. —Ghana (Akan)

Where there is an old man, one does not ask the advice of a young man. —Togo (Hoi)

An old man lying in the room is better than an old man lying in a grave. —Africa

The old man's mouth may be twisted, but not his words. —Zambia

The mouth of the elderly man is without teeth but never without words of wisdom.
—*East Africa (Kiswahili)*

Where there is an old man, nothing need go wrong.
—*East Africa (Kiswahili)*

The young do the fighting; the old ones do the peacemaking.
—*Ethiopia*

If a string of beads breaks in the presence of the elders, they are not lost.
—*Ghana (Twi)*

If you wish to be a real elder, you close your ears and your eyes.
—*Ghana (Akan)*

The elder does not listen to gossip over the fence.
—*Ghana (Akan, Twi)*

When consulting an elder, it is not proper to withhold information.
—*Africa*

An elder can be advised but never insulted.
—*Kenya (Agikuyu)*

Old people's talk is not scorned; they saw the sun first.
—*Africa*

Any elder who does not know how to sit on a stool sooner or later shall see it taken from underneath him.
—*Africa*

Where the elder comes to a stop, the younger
man catches up.                                    —*Benin, Nigeria, Togo (Yoruba)*

You can run quicker than an old man, but for his
wisdom and his words, you are behind.              —*Tanzania (Sukuma)*

An old calabash is still useful.                   —*Mali (Minyanka)*

However old the horse may be, it is still better than
new sandals.                                       —*Africa*

An old body is not hard to wash.                   —*Ghana (Akan)*

Grow old, body; the heart still remains.           —*Zimbabwe (Ndebele)*

The breaking day has wisdom; the falling day,
experience.                                        —*Zimbabwe (Ndanga)*

If you do not carry it on black hair, you will carry it
on gray hair.                                      —*Ghana (Twi)*

The tiger may get old, but his claws get sharper.  —*Haiti*

When tiger gets old, dog barks at him.             —*Africa*

An egg never sits on a hen.                        —*East Africa (Kiswahili)*

A new broom sweeps clean, but an old broom knows
the corners.                                       —*U.S. Virgin Islands*

If the new hoe want to know how tough the ground is,
make him ask the old hoe.                          —*Jamaica*

An old man running early in the morning is either
pursuing something, or something is pursuing him.

                                                   —*Africa*

Old dog don't bark for nothing. —*Antigua*

He who laughs at a scar has not received a wound.
—*East Africa (Kiswahili)*

One who has been pricked by a thorn values shoes.
—*East Africa (Kiswahili)*

The old woman has a reason for running in the rice
field. —*Côte d'Ivoire (Baule)*

If an old woman is chasing a rabbit, she has already killed
more than one. —*Burkina Faso (Mamprusi)*

An old woman cannot be frightened by marriage.
—*Senegal (Fulani)*

The mother of twins does not fear a huge penis.
—*Côte d'Ivoire (Baule)*

He who is stricken knows how to ward off the blow.
—*Kenya (Agikuyu)*

That which bit me yesterday and hurt me does not crawl
over me a second time. —*East Africa (Kiswahili)*

To see once is to see twice. —*South Africa (Zulu)*

He who has been bitten by a snake becomes scared by
the sight of a rope. —*Niger, Nigeria (Hausa)*

He who is already wet is not afraid of the rain. —*Ethiopia*

One does not run to the funeral of a person who died
by stumbling over a stone. —*Ghana (Akan)*

He who has seen a thousand does not praise a hundred.

—*Ghana (Twi)*

Those who have experienced nothing mistake the sound of weeping for singing. —*Ghana, Benin, Togo (Ewe)*

Nobody is born with teeth. —*Uganda (Ganda, Lugbara)*

Young yam can't make soup. —*Jamaica*

The young cannot teach tradition to the old.

—*Central Africa, East Africa, southern Africa (Bantu)*

A silly daughter teaches her mother how to bear children. —*Ethiopia*

You do not teach the paths of the forest to an old gorilla.

—*Congo*

Anywhere you find a road, people have passed there before. —*Africa*

Only the feet of the voyager know the path. —*East Africa*

The old elephant knows where to find water. —*South Africa*

If you follow an elephant, you do not lose your way.

—*Ghana (Akan)*

The man who goes ahead stumbles so that the man who follows may have his wits about him. —*Tanzania, Kenya (Bondei)*

Old hunters do not fall into traps. —*South Africa*

The one who falls in a ditch teaches others to be careful.

—*Benin, Nigeria, Togo (Yoruba)*

The tongue of experience holds the most truth. *—Egypt*

The dead gazelle teaches the live gazelle. *—Tanzania (Chagga)*

The teacher dies first. *—Uganda (Ganda, Lugbara)*

The wisdom of the dead prevents the old man from
making mistakes. *—Africa*

The old arrow is a model for the craftsman making a
new one. *—Ghana (Twi)*

You should make a new bucket while you still have the
old one. *—North Africa (Berber)*

Older the violin, sweeter the tune. *—Guyana, Belize*

The older the moon, the brighter it shine. *—Jamaica*

Only God is old. *—Kenya (Agikuyu)*

## ⬧ ADVICE AND COUNSEL

Do not ask advice from God and then pass by what
He said. *—Egypt*

Good advice is the second mother of a child. *—Africa*

If your grandfather informs you of trouble,
you shouldn't ask your father. *—Burkina Faso (Mamprusi)*

If you refuse the elder's advice, you will walk the
whole day. *—Tanzania (Ngoreme)*

The advice of the old is never overlooked. *—Kenya (Agikuyu)*

Give advice; if people do not listen, let adversity teach
them.
*—Ethiopia*

One who refused advice was later seen bleeding.
*—Mozambique, Zimbabwe (Shona)*

You can recognize a child who fails to take advice from
his bleeding wounds.
*—Lesotho*

She who ignores advice does not resist when being
prepared for burial.
*—Kenya (Agikuyu)*

It is useless to warn one who has made up his mind
*—Angola (Umbundu)*

I gave you advice; you tied it to some grass and tossed
it away; having done so, you lit a torch and went
about seeking it.
*—Nigeria (Efik)*

The only thing to do with good advice is to pass it on.
*—Uganda (Ganda)*

You do not counsel the wise; you do not slice meat for
a lion.
*—Ethiopia*

Even the clever one is advised.
*—Kenya, Uganda (Luhya)*

The stream won't be advised; therefore, its course
is crooked.
*—Cameroon*

A frustrated person will consult a madman for advice.
*—Africa*

A fly that has no one to advise it follows the corpse
into the grave.
*—Gambia*

Knowledge is not there at the beginning. —*Kenya (Agikuyu)*

All that is known is not told. —*Egypt*

Knowledge is like the ocean; no man's arms can
embrace it. —*East Africa (Kiswahili)*

Knowledge is like a garden: if it is not cultivated,
it cannot be harvested. —*Guinea*

Knowledge is never wasted. —*Gambia (Mandinka)*

He who does not know one thing knows another.

—*Kenya*

Knowledge is better than riches. —*Burundi*

Lack of knowledge is darker than night. —*Africa*

He to whom things are brought does not know the
length of the road. —*Namibia (Ovambo)*

Not to know is bad; not to want to know is worse.

—*Gambia*

He who asks questions cannot avoid the answers.

—*Cameroon*

He who asks questions hears the language or
gets interpretations. —*Nigeria (Efik)*

No one is without knowledge except him who asks
no questions. —*Central Africa (Fulfulde)*

If one does not know what to do, she does what
she knows.           *—Nigeria (Igbo)*

It is the forest clearer who knows the troubles caused
by trunks and wild animals.     *—Kenya (Agikuyu)*

The person who guards frogs knows best which frogs
are lame.         *—Gambia (Mandinka)*

If a fish comes out of the water and says the crocodile
has one eye, who will deny?     *—Nigeria (Igbo)*

Nobody can better describe to the bat what goes on in
the night period.     *—Africa*

No one knows how the water enters the coconut.

    *—Africa*

That which the ear has heard
and the eye has seen it is
useless for your mouth to
deny.     *—DRC (Mongo)*

Seeing excites knowing.   *—Africa*

Let him speak who has seen
with his eyes.     *—DRC*

It is the person who knows
how to shoot whom we put
on the track of an animal.

    *—Ghana (Akan)*

It is the hand that tied the lion that knows best how to
untie it.     *—Africa*

Only the wearer knows where the shoe pinches.    *—Brazil*

The shoe knows if the stocking has a hole.    *—Bahamas*

No one knows what goes on behind closed doors.

*—Zimbabwe*

Sleep in the house and you will know where it leaks.

*—Congo*

Only he who treads on the fire feels it.    *—Libya*

It is only the dead person who knows what the grave
is like.    *—Africa*

If one person does not know, another explains.

*—Ghana (Ashanti)*

Know yourself better than he does who speaks of you.

*—Senegal, Gambia (Wolof)*

The cow don't know the use of he tail till mosquito
season come.    *—Guyana*

Until a crab enters the cooking pot, it does not know that
there are two types of water.    *—Africa*

What you do not know you won't recognize.    *—Burundi*

What you don't know older than you.    *—Jamaica*

## ❋ USEFULNESS

A bird knows best whether its legs or wings are more
useful. *—Gambia (Mandinka)*

A basket with its bottom burst is useless.
*—Benin, Nigeria, Togo (Yoruba)*

What is not dead, don't dash it away. *—Jamaica*

Better to repair than to build anew. *—Niger, Nigeria (Hausa)*

Better to plaster an old wall than to build a new one.
*—Niger, Nigeria (Hausa)*

Patching makes the garment last; inattention made
one threadbare. *—Benin, Nigeria, Togo (Yoruba)*

Even if the drum does not sound well, we dance to it
all the same. *—Ghana (Twi)*

Even if the elephant is thin, its meat will fill a
hundred baskets. *—Ghana*

If a knife is blunt, it can still do to cut shea butter.
*—Ghana (Akan)*

The split tree still grows. *—Senegal, Gambia (Wolof)*

If the road is not good, there are still people on it.
*—Ghana*

Dirty water will put out fire. *—Jamaica*

The rotten sponge, we use it in times of need.

*—Ghana (Akan)*

An abandoned rag in one corner of the house will
one day be useful. *—Africa*

The old hoe is still a friend. *—Uganda (Ganda, Lugbara)*

Even though the cripple has nothing, he can at least
clap his hands. *—Ghana*

Though a tree does not bear fruit, it is not cut down.

*—Namibia (Ovambo)*

Though your coat is dirty, you do not burn it. *—Ghana (Twi)*

If there is nothing in the forest, there is at least stillness.

*—Ghana*

It is only the water that is spilled; the bowl is not broken!

*—Mauritania*

Try this bracelet. If it fits, wear it; if it hurts you,
throw it away, no matter how shiny. *—Niger, Nigeria (Hausa)*

Death
and
Afterlife

My uncle Tommy was ailing and in his eighties, but I was in disbelief when I felt his body and found no pulse. "Death is a visitor who will always take us by surprise" (Africa). He had told me he wanted none of the traditional ways of marking death— certainly no church ceremony—when we discussed the consequences of his refusing surgery that might have extended his life. He believed he had lived and "it is useless to be afraid of death" (Cameroon). However, recognizing that "funeral is for us all" (Tanzania), I held an informal gathering of relatives to say a final good-bye to Uncle Tommy.

On the other hand, Marcus, from a Rastafarian family, was shot dead at seventeen. His family and community were outraged at the manner of his passing: "Lion kills antelope, wolf kills sheep, but man kills man" (Eritrea, Ethiopia). His grandmother, in particular, grieved, because she did not expect to bury her son, let alone her grandson, even though she was aware that "the brown leaves are on the tree while the green ones are dropping" (Ghana).

I attended the set-up held for Marcus the night before his funeral. When I arrived, *kumina* drummers and dancers had already begun a ceremony intended to give Marcus a safe and speedy passage to the next world. From close to midnight until dawn, drums, shakers, and graters kept rhythm for ceremonial dancers, all women led by a queen. The drums summoned the spirits that possessed some of the dancers, and the queen performed rituals to communicate with the spirits and then dismiss them. Food was ritually offered to the unseen ones, because "a person who gives to the ancestors eats with them" (Tanzania).

The ceremony tapered off after the queen sprinkled raw white rum over the clothes in which Marcus would be buried. By then, Marcus's family seemed assured that the manner of his passing would not prevent his joining his ancestors, as "a tree cannot stand without roots"(DRC).

## ✳ DEATH AND DYING

It is the sea only that knows the bottom of the ship,
as God only knows the time of death.     *—Nigeria (Efik)*

The brown leaves are on the tree while the green ones
are dropping.     *—Ghana (Twi)*

Death is a visitor who will always take us by surprise.

*—Africa*

Lion kills antelope, wolf kills sheep, but man kills man.

*—Eritrea, Ethiopia (Kunama)*

Death does not discriminate and has no preference.

*—South Africa*

Death is a well everyone will drink from.     *—Africa*

Death is one ditch you cannot jump.

*—United States (South Carolina Gullah)*

Death is like a robe everyone has to wear.     *—Guinea (Mandingo)*

Death is in the leg: we walk with it.

*—Zimbabwe, South Africa (Tsonga)*

Death is like a thief. It never announces its visit.     *—Congo*

Death is not a sleeping room that can be entered and
come out of again.     *—Ghana (Ashanti)*

A person does not die twice.     *—Ghana (Akan)*

If you want to know what death is, look at sleep.

—*Ghana (Twi)*

No one can sleep as much as the dead. —*Ghana (Akan)*

Death is the greatest physician, which cures all diseases.

—*Nigeria (Igbo)*

When death arrives, illness is put to shame. —*Ghana (Akan)*

Dead man cannot run from a coffin. —*Barbados*

Strength does not prevent you from dying. —*Kenya (Agikuyu)*

Prayers and tears do not stop you from dying. —*Haiti*

Never mind how pumpkin vine run, it must dry up one day. —*Barbados, Guyana*

It is useless to be afraid of death.

—*Cameroon (Yaoundé)*

Death has the key to open the miser's chest. —*Ghana (Ashanti)*

When the gods want a dog to die, they simply numb his sense of smell.

—*Uganda (Ganda)*

Death needs a strong heart.           *—Uganda (Ganda, Lugbara)*

The goat says, "Nobody willingly walks to his own death."
*—Ghana*

If one could know where death resided, one would never
stop there.           *—Ghana (Ashanti)*

Death does not sound a trumpet.       *—Congo, Liberia*

When death holds something in its grip, life cannot
take it away.           *—Ghana (Akan)*

A dead body will not refuse decay.     *—East Africa (Kiswahili)*

As the grass cannot grow in the sky, so the dead cannot
look out of the grave into the road.
*—Benin, Nigeria, Togo (Yoruba)*

One must pay attention to the words of a dying person.
*—Kenya (Agikuyu)*

The mouth of the dead is respected.     *—Burundi (Rundi)*

A tree is best measured when it is down.     *—Nigeria*

When a dead tree falls, the woodpeckers profit from
its death.           *—Malawi*

Nobody mourns an unnoticed death.     *—Burundi*

Lie down and die, and you will see who really loves you.
*—Niger, Nigeria (Hausa)*

Whatever you love, death also loves.     *—Ghana*

Funeral is for us all.   *—Tanzania (Bena)*

At the funeral, one cries for the living and not for
the dead.   *—Nigeria (Igbo)*

If you are unable to give a funeral donation, you
dance funeral dances enthusiastically.   *—Ghana (Akan)*

The burial ceremonies are quite bothersome when
the dead calls for more attention than when he was alive.
*—Tanzania (Haya)*

The death of a bad person does not pain people.
*—Ghana (Akan)*

The death of the suicide cannot be avenged.
*—Ghana, Benin, Togo (Ewe)*

The thoughts after which a man killed himself were not
deliberated upon over only one night, but many nights.
*—Nigeria (Igbo)*

The dead are no longer terrible.   *—Angola (Umbundu)*

Death is like a spoiled child: it gets everything.   *—Namibia*

You travel on until you return home; you live on
until you return to earth.   *—Ethiopia*

Even the longest life ends in a grave.   *—Ghana (Ewe)*

The dead who are buried in shallow graves will haunt
the living.   *—Uganda (Buganda)*

## ✳ ANCESTORS

Youths look at the future, the elderly at the past; our ancestors live in the present. —*Kenya (Kalenjin, Luo)*

If we stand tall, it is because we stand on the backs of those who came before us. —*Benin, Nigeria, Togo (Yoruba)*

No matter how great a king, he still needs the voice of the ancestors. —*Africa*

A tree cannot stand without roots. —*DRC (Mayombe)*

A person who gives to the ancestors eats with them.

—*Tanzania*

## ❦ Acknowledgments

I thank all who had a hand in raising me—my grandfather Arthur Brown; my grandmothers, Adassa (Annie) Brown and Clementina McCalla; my parents, Ettle and Allan McCalla; and my aunt-mother Ethline McCalla—for their instinctive grasp of the language of proverbs.

I thank Helen and Mervyn Morris, who offered love, insight, encouragement, and access to Mervyn's collection of Caribbean proverbs. I also thank Ann Walmsley Farquhar for sending me a book of Guyanese proverbs originally published in 1902. I appreciate the support of caring family members connected by blood and spirit: my sons Pierre and Hilaire Sobers, my daughter-in-law Alison Irvine-Sobers, my cousins Hope McNish and Dawn Grant, my longtime friends Jean McCulloch and Cecile Pike, who offered words of advice and encouragement, respected occasions when I needed solitude, and provided diversions when I needed to relax so I could renew. Many thanks also to my aunts Pearl Bailey and Dawn Charlton, and cousins Sadie Fraser and Joyce and Neville Rhone, who contributed to the section introductions their memories of our common ancestors.

I am particularly grateful to my coauthor, Askhari, for her inspiration, her commitment, and her sister-hood.

—Yvonne McCalla Sobers

My absolute love to my parents, Janie Ruth McClellan Johnson and Carver Lorenzo Johnson, for being re-sponsible, community- and spirit-centered parents who continue to teach me the meaning of reciprocity, loyalty, and unconditional love. i still love and re-member Aunt Weez, Grandma Addie, Granddaddy Henry, Grandpa Sam, Uncle Alton, Aunt Pawnee, and Aunt Dret. Your words stay with me. Aunt Tish, Aunt Binner, and Aunt Jackie: i love listening to you.

My deepest gratitude to and respect for my co-author, Yvonne (Nothango), for her sisterhood, strength, passion, patience, and commitment to for-ward motion. My regards and thanks to the following: Khary Johnson, Kendra Corr Roberson (Yara), Bet-tina Byrd Giles, William Asim Muhammad, Ericka Wright, Joanetta Jarman (Anim), Sharifa Wip, Eddie Luster, Heather Martin, Akinyele Umoja, and Boatema Sonyika; also the following student assistants for technical assistance: Theodore Foster, Alexis Mor-ris, and Kimberly Rodgers.

My unrelenting love to my family (blood and love)—a family that never stops giving of itself in myr-iad ways. Let it be known: i appreciate you; i value you; and you are mentioned in my daily prayers/chants, in the hope my love and gratitude will make a way back to you in tangible ways.

—Askhari Johnson Hodari

*Lifelines* is truly a community/village/family collaboration. Therefore, both authors wish to acknowledge all the griots, *djeli*, sages, chiefs, kings, queens, and initiates who happily and generously contributed proverbs to this collection. We value the contributions of the Archbishop Desmond Tutu and artist Katie Yamasaki. We also acknowledge the following members of de Griot Space Writing Workshop for thoughtful critiques of this work: Kim Banton, Lynn Craig, Ronald Davis, Quentin Huff, Michelle Yvonne Lee, Collier Lunn, Tzynya Pinchback, and Andrew Reeves. In addition, we acknowledge the following members of the Broadway Books staff: Hallie Falquet, Hilary Roberts, Caroline Sill, and Jennifer Robbins. We appreciate everyone who has been waiting for this book. If you have purchased this book, a part of the authors' proceeds go toward Save Africa's Children. The authors also offer appreciation and thanks to our agent, Rita Rosenkranz, and our initial editor, Christian Nwachukwu, for providing a peaceful and positive bridge between the idea of *Lifelines* and these pages that turn.

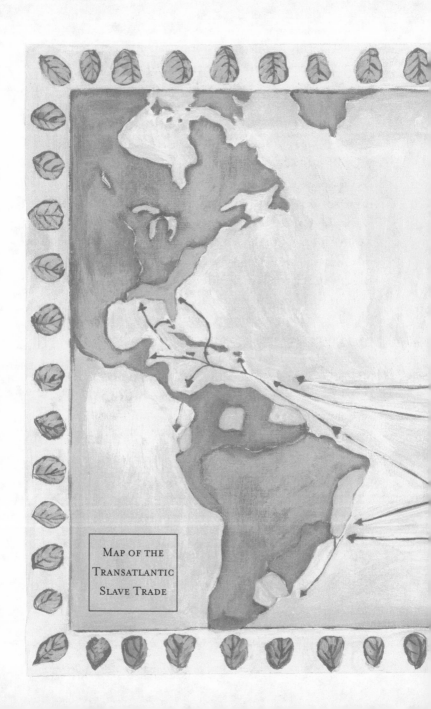

MAP OF THE
TRANSATLANTIC
SLAVE TRADE

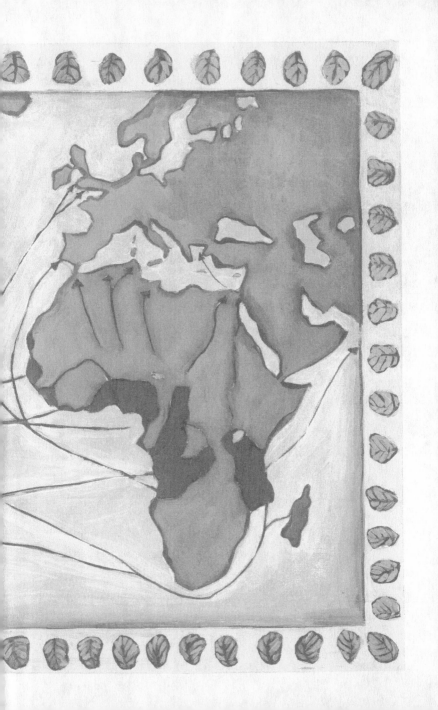

# ❧ Bibliography

> The darkest thing about Africa has always been our
> ignorance of it.
>
> —George Kimble

A detailed bibliography has been included to reference
works and, as important, to encourage further exploration
of African proverbs and culture.

Abdulai, D. (2000). *African Proverbs: Wisdom of the Ages.* Accra,
Ghana: Dawn of a New Day Publications.

Adelekan, T. (2004 ). *African Wisdom: 101 Proverbs from the Moth-
erland.* Valley Forge, PA: Judson Press.

Ademola, K. (2000). *More African Proverbs.* Lagos, Nigeria:
Pocket Gifts.

Anderson, I. (1972). *Jamaica Proverbs and Sayings.* Dublin: Irish
University Press.

Appiah, P., and K. Appiah. (2001). *Bu Me Be: Akan Proverbs.*
Accra, Ghana: Center for Intellectual Renewal.

Ayele, N. (1998). *Wit and Wisdom from Ethiopia.* Hollywood: Tsehai Publishers and Distributors.

Baptise, R. (1993). *Trini Talk: A Dictionary of Words and Proverbs of Trinidad and Tobago.* Trinidad, West Indies: Caribbean Information Systems and Services.

Beckwith, M. (1925). *Jamaica Proverbs.* New York: Negro Universities Press.

Beckwith, M. (1970). *Jamaica Proverbs.* Westport, CT: Greenwood Press.

Burton, R. (1969). *Wit and Wisdom from West Africa; Or, A Book of Proverbial Philosophy, Idioms, Enigmas, and Laconisms.* Cheshire, CT: Biblo & Tannen Booksellers & Publishers.

Calana, Z. (2003). *Xhosa Proverbs and Metaphors.* Roggebaai, South Africa: Kwela Books.

Christaller, J. (1990). *Three Thousand Six Hundred Ghanaian Proverbs (From the Asante and Fante Languages).* Lewiston, NY: Edwin Mellen Press.

Cordry, H. (2005). *The Multicultural Dictionary of Proverbs : Over 20,000 Adages from More Than 120 Languages, Nationalities and Ethnic Groups.* Jefferson, NC: McFarland & Company.

Cotter, G. (1992). *Proverbs and Sayings of the Oromo People of Ethiopia and Kenya with English Translations.* Lewiston, NY: Edwin Mellen Press.

Cross, V. (1994). *Black Folk, Wit, Wisdom and Sayings.* Kansas City, MO: Andrews and McMeel.

Dalfovo, A. (1997). *Lugbara Wisdom*. Pretoria, South Africa: Unisa Press.

Dicks, I. (2006). *Wisdom of the Yawo People: Yawo Proverbs and Stories*. Zamba, Madawi: Kachere Series, University of Malawi.

Elkhadem, S. (1987). *Egyptian Proverbs and Popular Sayings*. York, England: York Press.

Feldman, R., and C. Voelke. (1992). *A World Treasury of Folk Wisdom*. San Francisco: HarperCollins.

Fonge, M. (1997). *Discover Life's Treasures Hidden in African Proverbs: Where Village Is the Foundation*. Houston, TX: LeBock Publishing.

Ibekwe, P. (1998). *Wit & Wisdom of Africa: Proverbs from Africa & the Caribbean*. Trenton, NJ: Africa World Press.

Jennings, C. (1996). *As the Old Folks Usta' Say . . . : Black Proverbs, Sayings, and Folk-Wit*. Los Angeles: Sepia House Publishers.

Knappert, J. (1989). *The A–Z of African Proverbs*. London: Karnak House.

Kwayana, E. (1997). *Gang Gang: Thirty African Guyanese Proverbs*. Georgetown, Guyana: Red Thread Women's Press.

Lambie, N. (1972). *Where Continents Meet: African Proverbs*. New York: John Day Company.

Leslau, C., and W. Leslau. (1985). *African Proverbs.* White Plains, NY: Peter Pauper Press.

Ley, G. (1999). *African Proverbs.* New York: Hippocrene Books.

McCormick, M. (1992). *A Collection of African Proverbs.* New York: Stone Street Press.

Malungu, C., and C. Banda. (2007). *Understanding Organizational Sustainability Through African Proverbs: Insights for Leaders and Facilitators.* Washington, DC: Pact Publications.

Merrick, G. (1969). *Hausa Proverbs.* New York: Negro Universities Press.

Mieder, W. (1997). *The Prentice-Hall Encyclopedia of World Proverbs: A Treasury of Wit and Wisdom Through the Ages.* New York: MJF Books.

Mokitimi, M. (1997). *The Voice of the People: Proverbs of the Basotho.* Pretoria, South Africa: Unisa Press.

Musere, J. (1999). *African Proverbs and Proverbial Names.* Los Angeles: Ariko Publications.

Okwelume, O. (2004). *Drumbeats of Black Africa: A Collection of African Proverbs.* Ibadan, Nigeria: Spectrum Books.

Omole, W. (1998). *Collection of African Proverbs & Usages* (Vol. 1). Ibadan, Nigeria: Molley Publishers Limited.

Opoku, K. (1997). *Hearing and Keeping: Akan Proverbs.* Accra, Ghana: Asempa Publishers.

Owomoyela, O. (2005). *Yoruba Proverbs.* Lincoln: University of Nebraska Press.

Scheffler, A. (1997). *Let Sleeping Dogs Lie, and Other Proverbs from Around the World.* Hauppauge, New York: Barron's Educational Series.

Schipper, M. (2003). *Never Marry a Woman with Big Feet: Women in Proverbs from Around the World.* New Haven, CT: Yale University Press.

Schipper, M. (1993). *Source of All Evil: African Proverbs and Sayings on Women.* Chicago: Ivan R. Dee.

Stewart. J. (1997). *African Proverbs and Wisdom.* New York: Kensington Publishing.

Stone, J. (2006). *The Routledge Book of World Proverbs.* New York: Routledge.

Trottman, J. (2006). *The Proverbs of Guyana Explained.* London: Bogle L'Ouverture Press.

Wanjohi, G. (2001). *Under One Roof: Gikuyu Proverbs.* Nairobi, Kenya: Pauline Publications Africa.

West African Museums Programme (2004). *Mandinka Proverbs and Sayings from the Gambia.* Dakar, Senegal.

Znyembezi, C. (1954). *Zulu Proverbs.* Johannesburg, South Africa: Witwatersrand University Press.

Zona, G. (1994). *The Soul Would Have No Rainbow If the Eyes Had No Tears.* New York: Simon & Schuster.

It is the person who knows how to shoot whom we put on the track of an animal.

—Ghana

## ABOUT THE AUTHORS

**Yvonne McCalla Sobers** is a Jamaican who writes fiction and nonfiction. She is a graduate of the University of the West Indies and taught English and history for much of her career. Yvonne lives in Kingston, travels the Americas and the Caribbean, and worked for many years in Britain and in Ghana. Living in Africa helped her identify the roots of proverbs that she learned as a child, when she first fell in love with these sayings. She is the author of the cookbook *Delicious Jamaica! Vegetarian Cuisine* (Book Publishing Company, 1996). To contact Yvonne McCalla Sobers, please write to sobersy@yahoo.com.

**Askhari Johnson Hodari, Ph.D.**, a Black Studies practitioner, received degrees from Spelman College and Howard University. Above all, she values the education her family and community share with her (usually at the dinner or kitchen table). Although she frequently visits countries in Africa, the Americas, and the Caribbean, Hodari makes her home in Birmingham, Alabama, a home of the civil- and human-rights movements. Hodari is the author of *The African Book of Names* (Health Communications, Inc., February 2009) and the moderator of de Griot Space, an online writing workshop (http://groups.yahoo.com/group/deGriotSpace/). To contact Askhari Johnson Hodari, please write to writedrhodari@gmail.com.

Note: Please share your thoughts on our proverb selections by e-mailing us at daughtersofexperience@gmail.com.

## ABOUT THE ILLUSTRATOR

**Katie Yamasaki** is a muralist, illustrator, and fine artist in Brooklyn, New York. www.katieyamasaki.com

www.lifelines.proverbs.com